A YEAR OF JUBILEE

A YEAR OF JUBILEE

Celebrating fifty years of God's grace
bestowed upon a little country church
on the northern borders of
Burlington, Ontario

Mark B. Hudson

Trinity Baptist Church
Declaring the whole counsel of God (Acts 20:27)
1972–2022

HOUSE TO HOUSE, *an imprint of*

hesedandemet.com

H&E Publishing, Peterborough, Ontario, Canada

© 2022 Mark B. Hudson. All rights reserved. This book may not be reproduced, in whole or in part, without written permission from the publishers.

Cover, editing and book design by Janice Van Eck

A Year of Jubilee: Celebrating Fifty Years of God's Grace Bestowed Upon A Little Country Church on the Northern Borders of Burlington, Ontario
Mark B. Hudson

ISBN 978-1-77484-074-0 (paperback)
ISBN 978-1-77484-075-7 (e-book)

*To all those who poured their heart and soul into serving the Lord
and one another at Trinity through the years,
particularly to my beloved wife,
Merry-Lynn,
who I would place very near the top of that list,
though she would, undoubtedly, insist otherwise.*

◇◇◇◇◇◇◇◇

Contents

	Foreword by Kirk M. Wellum	ix
	Preface	xiii
	Acknowledgements	xv
1	William E. Payne: The years of preparation, 1938–1972	1
2	Setting down roots: The 1970s	13
3	Early growth and its challenges: The 1980s	45
4	Coming of age: The 1990s	59
5	A time of expansion: The 2000s	93
6	A decade of testing: The 2010s	113
7	Winding up the first half-century: 2020–2022	157

Appendices

1	Founding members of Trinity Baptist Church	181
2	Key positions of service & leadership	183
3	Missionary support	189
4	Firsts, buildings & church support	191
5	Motto texts	195
6	Church anniversary speakers	197
7	Cradle roll: Babies born at Trinity	201
8	What in the world happened in the….	205
9	What is a Reformed Baptist church?	207

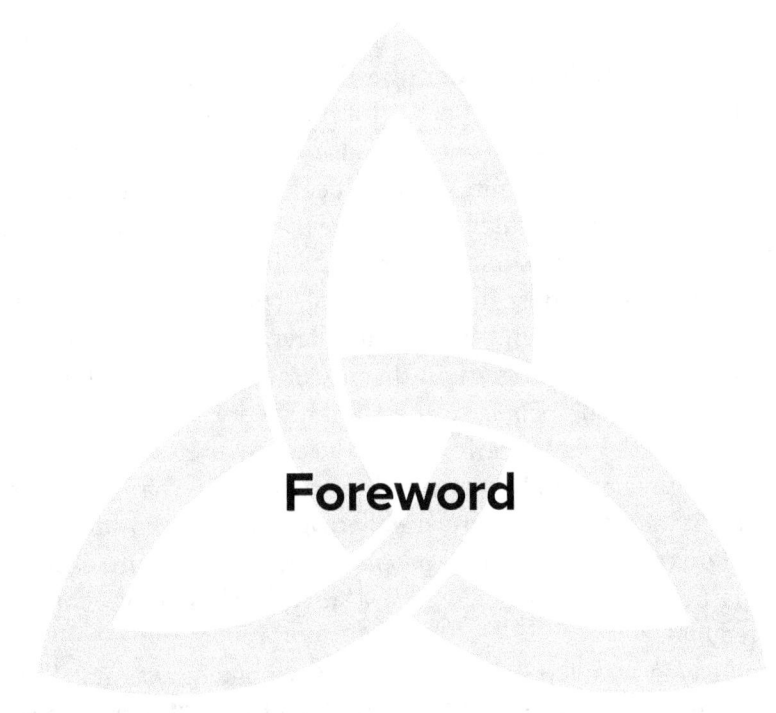

Foreword

Trinity Baptist Church (Trinity), in Burlington, Ontario, will always have a special place in my life. I attended the church during a formative period in my life where I heard the gospel faithfully preached week after week and, after I became a Christian, I was baptized there and given some of my earliest opportunities to preach the Scriptures in anticipation of God's call on my life and future ministry.

Reading Mark Hudson's history of the church from its inception in October 1972 through to June 2022 brought back a flood of memories and deep gratitude for all the Lord has done through this church. I have known Mark (and his late wife Merry-Lynn) for many years and his love for and knowledge of the church as a church member and church leader, eminently qualifies him tell the story of God's sovereign grace in the establishment, growth and influence of Trinity over the past fifty years.

As it happens, my part in the story began when my parents took our family to Calvary Baptist Church where, as a teen, I sat under the ministry of Pastor Bill Payne. A few years later, along with my parents and brothers, I attended the newly formed Trinity Baptist Church meeting at Trefoil

Lodge in Burlington. The impact of Pastor Payne's ministry on my life and ministry is incalculable. The older I get the more thankful I have become for his theological balance and powerful preaching of the whole counsel of God. But as I read this history, I was also reminded that so many other things happened during Trinity's first half century; events and the people connected to them that would fade with the passage of time were it not for Mark's detailed and fascinating account.

As with any church over the years, people come and go, and that was certainly true of Trinity. But in the early days, I remember there was a definite pattern to these migrations that became more apparent over time. The Lord would bring people to the church where they would hear the doctrines of God's grace clearly taught and then, after a time, he would send them elsewhere and they would take what they had learned with them. In that way, the gospel spread and proved a blessing to others. Mark's story contains the names of many people connected to Trinity, each one of them a part of the story of God's grace, a story that has not yet come to its appointed end.

Pastor Payne was Trinity's founding pastor, but he was not the last. Mark recounts the long and faithful ministry of Carl Muller, who served as a pastoral assistant before becoming the pastor after Bill Payne's death. Like his predecessor, Carl steadfastly preached the gospel of God's grace and never stopped urging his listeners to surrender themselves to the Lord Jesus Christ. Carl and I went to seminary together and although we have served in different churches and Christian ministries, I know that we will never forget the ministry and influence of Pastor Payne and Trinity in our service of Christ. In many ways, they have given us the strength and resolve to press on no matter what the difficulties knowing that God is in control and His purposes will stand and His wisdom will be vindicated.

Trinity also has a history of generosity that included supporting many churches in a variety of ways. From providing leadership through the Fellowship for Reformation and Pastoral Studies (now the Grace Pastors' Fellowship) to the Carey Conference, the support of missionaries and church plants, the distribution of literature and sermons and involvement with seminaries like Toronto Baptist Seminary (TBS), Trinity was exemplary. In fact, I believe it will not be until the great and final day when we all stand before the Lord that we will learn all that He has done through this assembly of His people in all its ups and downs for however long He chooses to keep its lampstand burning.

Mark Hudson's book chronicles the first fifty years, but since he put down his pen (or more likely stopped typing on his keyboard) time marches on. At the end of his account, he relates how in recent days Trinity Baptist Church has a new pastor, TBS graduate Josh Mills, who will lead the church forward into the future. It is my prayer that many will read and spiritually profit from Mark's wonderfully interesting and edifying account of Trinity's past and, as they do, they will discover afresh what led to the founding of the church and what holds the key to its continued usefulness until the return of our Lord. I pray that Trinity will always be a place where the whole counsel of God is proclaimed in a winsome way with the biblical and theological balance that was so important to those who laid its foundation fifty years ago.

Kirk M. Wellum
Principal, Toronto Baptist Seminary
September 3, 2022

Preface

On the evening of Sunday, October 2, 1977, Merry-Lynn, myself and our three-month-old daughter Leslie, went in search of a church pastored by a man called William Payne. People said it lay somewhere in the countryside north of Burlington on Appleby Line. In those days, Appleby Line was a small, little travelled stretch of road with only a railway crossing and, north of Upper Middle Road, had but a single stop sign at Dundas Street. It was barren, dark and, at the time, it seemed an endless stretch of nothing going nowhere. At several points we felt the church, if it existed, had been missed and the prudent thing was to turn around. We journeyed on a little further until we came to "the gulley," a place where the edges of the road seem to drop off into dark depths of who-knows-what, and decided, if we ever emerged, we would turn around and go home. As we crested the hill on the far side looking for a place to turn, Merry-Lynn noticed some lights through the trees. We rounded the bend and saw the profile of an old, red brick church with a few cars in its parking lot. Assuming this to be our destination, we pulled in, got out and walked cautiously through the front door. The warmth of the greetings we received, the fullness of the congregational singing and the beauty of the Word preached, told us this was to be our new church home; it remained that for the next forty-three years.

The life of a true church of Jesus Christ is, in the most fundamental way, always in the hands of the sovereign God of Scripture. He plants, builds, sustains and blesses each local congregation according to His own providential mercy and plan. Some enjoy long periods of peaceful ministry, while others may face lengthy trials of fire and persecution. The life of some congregations spans many decades, while others come and go with a brevity only the Lord can understand. Whatever the path, His children learn to trust and follow Him, as they faithfully proclaim the saving gospel of Jesus Christ to a world of resistance and opposition.

Believers are humbled by His willingness to use mortal beings in His day-to-day workings, but they understand and confess that the effectiveness and spiritual impact of any church lies undeniably in the hands of, and under the direction and guidance of, the Holy Spirit. Remaining open to His leading and enabling will ultimately lead to serving His purposes.

As in other areas of life, church families like to recognize special occasions for celebration and thanksgiving. A favourite is that of highlighting anniversaries. These offer a special opportunity to thank the Lord for His ongoing faithfulness and mercy. Though some churches in Southern Ontario have been in existence for over 200 years, Trinity, based on such a timeline, has barely reached young adulthood. Nonetheless, being kept for fifty years in the service of the Lord is a significant number and certainly worth a word of celebration. In that time He has met every need, taught many essential lessons and maintained the light of gospel truth burning brightly. The prayer of the congregation is that future generations of believers will continue to be granted the great privilege of worshipping the Lord at Trinity.

God raised up Trinity Baptist Church by confronting a simple pastor with a choice: give up his convictions regarding biblical truth and stay or go elsewhere and preach and teach what he believed the Bible truly taught. In choosing the latter, he followed the leading of the Spirit of God and, by faith and trust in the Lord to do all things well, took on the challenge of a new church plant. Now, fifty years on, it is appropriate to look back at how the Lord has blessed that decision. It is, in a very tangible way, the end of Trinity's *Year of Jubilee* and so praise is given to God for overseeing all things for the good of His people and the glory of His name for half a century…and counting.

Acknowledgements

Most of the information recorded (unless otherwise noted) has been gleaned from church bulletins, minutes of board and member meetings, the personal writings of Pastor William Payne and Pastor Carl Muller, first-hand accounts of members and adherents and forty-three years of personal experience. There have been at least three previous histories of Trinity produced: *Beginnings*, written for the church's 25th anniversary in 1997; *A Time to Remember*, written at the time of the dedication of the new church addition in 2004; "*Declaring the Whole Counsel of God,*" produced by Dr. Michael Haykin to celebrate the church's 40th anniversary in 2012. There have also been newspaper, journal and magazine articles that offer interesting summaries of specific time periods in the church's development and growth.

Selections from these publications have been included and referenced where possible. An entire chapter from "*Declaring the Whole Counsel of*

God" has been included, in lightly edited form, with the kind permission of Dr. Michael Haykin.[1]

There is a technical side to publishing that requires the expertise of people with literary, artistic and grammatical skills. My thanks go out to Janice Van Eck who took the transcript and turned it into a book! She oversaw all the practical elements of publication; her professional skills have been highlighted once again. Special thanks to Hetty Payne for reviving her proofreading skills and checking through this volume on short notice —much appreciated. There are a few photographs included; they were gratefully received and, I trust, are properly credited. Thanks as well to Kirk Wellum, principal of Toronto Baptist Seminary and a member of one of the founding families of Trinity, for his willingness to read the manuscript and write the Foreword.

I would like to thank the Trinity board of elders and deacons for allowing me the opportunity to tackle this project on behalf of the congregation, both past and present. As a confirmed math teacher, there seem to be way too many words and not near enough numbers for my comfort level in this volume. However, I trust the Lord will bless this book to the hearts of those that read it. My hope is that the Lord's never-failing sustaining grace will be seen and appreciated in every aspect of the writing. It is really all about His work with His people in His church according to His plans and purposes. The people of Trinity would want it no other way.

---

[1] "Chapter 2: William E. Payne: the years of preparation, 1938–1972" in Michael A.G. Haykin, *'Declaring the Whole Counsel of God'* (Burlington, ON: Trinity Baptist Church, 2012), 21–30.

1

William E. Payne: The years of preparation

1938–1972

◇◇◇◇◇◇◇◇

All the way my Saviour leads me;
What have I to ask beside?
Can I doubt His tender mercy,
Who through life has been my Guide?
Heav'nly peace, divinest comfort,
Here by faith in Him to dwell!
For I know, whate'er befall me,
Jesus doeth all things well.

FANNY CROSBY

Canadians, it has been said, do not relish heroes. As Bill Payne once noted, "Canada is hardly a country of the sensational and the dramatic!"[1] Quite differently from those peoples who have played major roles in shaping our national character—the French, British and Americans—our history has given us a predilection for the ordinary. We have never had such hero-producing or hero-revealing events as a revolution or a national revival. Great Britain, France and the United States have all experienced the former and the larger-than-life figures in those revolutions. The nearest we have come to such have been the rebellions of 1837, which, as Charles Taylor noted, "are notable mainly for their ineptitude."[2] Nor has there ever been a national revival. Both the British Isles and America have known the blessing of such, while France experienced the extraordinary impact of the gospel during the period of the Reformation, when the Reformed faith grew from a handful of believers in the early 1520s to two million or so by the late 1560s. Revolutions and revivals are peopled by remarkable figures, and given our lack of the former, it is easy to think we have not had the latter. But we have: as Taylor goes on to observe, it is clear that "We have produced some remarkable people whose qualities often verge on the heroic."[3] And in the history of the Baptist community in Ontario during the past 200 years this is most definitely the case. Here one thinks of such men as R.A. Fyfe and D.A. McGregor in the nineteenth century—and, in his own way and for those who knew him, the founding pastor of Trinity Baptist Church, William Edward Payne.

Early days in Liverpool[4]

Bill Payne, as he was affectionately known, was born in Knowsley, just outside Liverpool, England, on April 16, 1938, and as a result would be known as a "Scouse" in the British Isles. Bill never lost the distinctive tones of his Liverpudlian accent. He was the third son of Thomas Lamb Payne and

---

[1] W.E. Payne, "The Reformation Movement Among Baptists in Ontario," *Reformation Canada* 8.1 (Spring 1985): 12.
[2] Charles Taylor, *Six Journeys: A Canadian Pattern* (Toronto: House of Anansi Press Ltd., 1977), i.
[3] Taylor, *Six Journeys*, ii.
[4] What follows is Hetty Payne's biographical sketch of her husband's life up until 1972, which Michael A.G. Haykin edited and supplemented in parts: "William Edward Payne—The Early Years" in Michael A.G. Haykin, ed., *William E. Payne: A Memoir* (Burlington, ON: Joshua Press, 1997), 6–15. Used with permission of H.M. Payne.

Bill & Hetty Payne

his wife Hannah. In the early years of their marriage Thomas had to leave Hannah in England to go to Africa to seek work, as he could not find a job in England at that time. Up to this point in his life he had attended church with Hannah, but upon his return Thomas ceased going to church completely and never showed any further interest in spiritual things. Bill's mother also stopped going to church, although she did try to influence her sons to go to Sunday School at St. George's Anglican Church. Without any real encouragement from home, however, they soon stopped and any interest in spiritual things was quenched.

During his teen years, Bill attended Prescott Grammar School where he became enamoured with sports, especially soccer. He was on the school team and eventually became its captain. His other love was cycling, and he would be out every weekend with a club of young people going into Wales or around the North of England. In all of this, there was no thought of God and no time for God in his life. Toward the end of his school years, Bill was seen by a scout from the Everton Football Club and later received a card asking him to come for a trial for their junior team, which seemed to Bill like the fabulous realization of a dream. But God had other plans, for while Bill had been filling his life with sports, circumstances around him had been changing.

"A new creation"

One of Bill's friends, Malcolm Fenton, who was a few years older than Bill, was also an avid soccer player and was on a team connected with the Liverpool Football Club. Bill looked up to Malcolm and thought he "had it made"—he had a career in soccer. However, one day Malcolm quit soccer and started going to church. Bill would see him leaving for church every Sunday with a big Bible under his arm, accompanied by his mother. Bill could not understand it, but it compelled him to stop and assess his own life. Although he had left school and started working at the Liverpool Savings Bank, and was still involved in sports, he was deeply dissatisfied. Then, an even stranger thing happened: his mother, who was great friends with Mrs. Fenton, started to go to church with her. There was a distinct change in his mother's life—she too began reading her Bible and going to church not only Sundays, but during the week as well. God brought Hannah to saving faith, for from that time on she obviously trusted God and walked with Him. She also began to encourage Bill to go to church with her.

Seeing the changes in the life of his mother and his friend, Bill began to wonder if "something was going on in this church." He knew certain things he was doing were wrong, but he had no idea how to better his life and relinquish these bad habits. He had no thoughts of God, yet he was curious about this church and he felt drawn to go with his mother to find out what this change in her life and Malcolm's life was all about.

So, one Sunday Bill accompanied his mother to Calvary Independent Baptist Church to hear the minister, Reverend A.E. Chillington.[5] For the very first time in his life, he heard the gospel preached. He heard of Christ's death on the cross for his sins, and that he was a sinner. He heard of his all-surpassing need to flee to Christ for salvation. It was all new to him; he had ever heard anything like this before. When he went home, he found he could not stop thinking about the Bible and what it said. He could not wait to get back to the church the following Sunday to hear more. God's plan for his life was being worked out, but Bill did not realize it.

Over the following weeks and months, Bill sat under the sound preaching of Pastor Chillington, and as Bill studied the Bible, God worked in his life. Eventually on February 13, 1955, when Bill was sixteen years old, he asked God to forgive his sins and cleanse him anew. He gave his life to God. One of Bill's favourite verses was 2 Corinthians 5:17: "Therefore, if anyone is in Christ, he is a new creation; old things have passed away; behold all things have become new." This was very much Bill's own experience. All the seeking after fullness of life in cycling and soccer was gone. Put away forever was the offer from Everton Football Club, and his life turned around completely.

Maturing in Christ

Bill simply could not get enough of God's Word. He was at every meeting possible at the church, trying to learn more of the God he had never known until then. He started reading Christian literature, although he had no idea what he should be reading. Soon he was giving his testimony publicly at meetings and it became obvious he had a gift for speaking. Pastor Chilllington, who had encouraged many of his young people to go into full-time service, gave Bill many opportunities to speak. When he was

---

[5] For a note regarding some background on Pastor Chillington, see Michael A.G. Haykin, ed., *'Declaring the Whole Counsel of God'* (Burlington, ON: Trinity Baptist Church, 2012), 93–94.

eighteen year old, he had his first outside speaking engagement. This was at a Nurses Fellowship in Liverpool. He spoke on the love of God, and, as he came to the end, he realized he did not know how to finish, so he looked up at the them said, "That's your lot," and sat down!

The years spent at Calvary Church were a blessing to Bill as a young Christian. He grew and matured under the faithful exposition of God's Word. A special bond developed between Bill and Pastor Chillington. The older man had faced his own battles in the Christian life. He was a self-taught man who in his early years had prepared his sermons outside of his home in the street under a lamppost, not being allowed to study inside his house. Bill came to love and respect Pastor Chillington and looked on him as his "father in the Lord." Pastor Chillington also knew many of the great preachers of that day and had them speak at the church. Thus, Bill had opportunity to hear many of them, including one of the most remarkable preachers of the twentieth century, Dr. Martyn Lloyd-Jones.

It was at Calvary Church that Bill met his future wife Hetty Stephenson, who had attended Calvary since the age of three and had been converted at age thirteen. As they got to know each other and fell in love, Bill and Hetty discovered they shared a desire to serve the Lord wherever He led. Together they developed a real interest in the Middle East, especially for the Muslim people. First, though, Bill had to complete his National Service (two years in the army) and Hetty had to finish her nurses training.

For Bill the two years in the army was a time of spiritual growth and testing. He was stationed at Grays, Essex, in a small medical first-aid post attached to a large camp. But before his posting, he had to do twelve weeks training in a larger camp at Colchester. In typical "Bill style" he determined to nail his colours to the mast right away. He later stated it was one of the hardest things he had done, to kneel by his bed on that first night and pray in the barracks full of non-Christians. But God honoured his stand and Bill won the respect of many of his fellow soldiers.

During his two years in the army, Bill was helped by a young pastor, Rev. Bundock, in the Baptist church in Grays. The pastor and his wife took Bill under their wing. They opened their house to Bill, and he spent many happy hours there, discussing the Bible or babysitting their two young boys. He continued to speak and preach wherever he could. In his spare time, Bill started to tackle New Testament Greek, with a view to Bible school. His aim to go to the Middle East never faltered. It is obvious from his correspondence to Hetty at this time that Bill was considering going to Spurgeon's College but Pastor Chillington advised against this move. Bill finished his National Service a stronger more mature Christian and ready for the next challenge of finding the right Bible School.

Studying at Toronto Baptist Seminary

On returning to Liverpool, Bill took a job at the Liverpool Savings Bank, while waiting for Hetty to finish her training as a nurse. By this time, Hetty and Bill had been engaged for two and a half years. They were subsequently married on a beautiful sunny day in August 1959. They were still seeking the Lord's will regarding the mission field, but they had no clear direction. They certainly did not think of leaving England for training, but once again God had his plans. Dr. H.C. Slade, pastor of Jarvis Street Baptist Church in Toronto, Canada, as well as the president of its Seminary, had come over to speak at Calvary and Bill was at the meeting (Hetty was working). At the end of the service, Dr. Slade said he felt there was a young man in the service who was interested in training and, if so, he should speak to him. Well, Bill wanted Bible training, but in Canada? That was much too far away! He went home and told Hetty about the meeting and then they put it out of their minds—but God's purposes were not to be thwarted.

Only six weeks later, Bill and Hetty were on their way across the Atlantic to Toronto Baptist Seminary (TBS) on Jarvis Street. They had tried to dismiss Canada from their minds, but God kept bringing it back and removing all obstacles they put up—until they were convinced this was God's will for them. They arrived at the seminary eager to learn, but with preconceived ideas in some areas. One area was prophecy. Their home church was dispensational, pretribulational and premillennial, but the seminary took a decidedly amillennial position. This was totally new to Bill and he thought it "heretical." He even declared they would have to go back to England. He came to realize he was reacting too strongly. After all, his professors, men like Dr. Geoff Adams[6] and Dr. G.B. Fletcher were godly men who had studied the Bible. Maybe, he thought, he should stay and study and learn. Besides, he was convinced it had been God's will for he and Hetty to come to Canada, so they had better stay. Dr. Fletcher, whom Bill and Hetty grew to love in the Lord, was a solid Calvinist and taught it clearly in his

---

[6] For Dr. Adams' life and ministry, see Michael A.G. Haykin, ed., *Acorns to Oaks, The Primacy and Practice of Biblical Theology: A Festschrift for Dr. Geoff Adams* (Dundas, ON: Joshua Press, 2003).

classes. Again, Bill had never heard Calvinism taught before; it was all new to him.[7] Over the four years as he studied Bill became convinced of the doctrines of Calvinism, but in his head only.

During his first year, Bill was called to minister at Central Baptist Church, a small congregation in Toronto. This proved to be a tremendous learning experience as he had to preach every Sunday and lead the midweek prayer meeting, as well as do his seminary studies. God undertook in a marvelous way to uphold him spiritually and physically. His academic marks never slipped. He was top of his class every year, even though he had the full responsibility of the church as well.

The time at seminary was extremely busy and profitable. Dr. Fletcher, for instance, who taught systematic theology, not only gave Bill a strong theological base, but also was a marvellous example of a godly Christian man. Dr. C.D. Cole, whom Bill met in his first year, was another man who left a deep impression on Bill. His love and communion with his Lord were so obvious. There were many others at the seminary who, through their teaching, molded Bill and "fine-tuned" the gifts God had given him.

All through seminary, Bill and Hetty kept their desire to go to the mission field in front of them and during the final year the question became what missionary society they should apply to. Being Baptist, they naturally thought about a Baptist mission. A few months before the end of seminary, a representative from the Bible Baptist Fellowship came to the seminary to present the work of their organization. Since they were working among Muslims, Bill decided to talk to the representative. One problem was Bill's position on prophecy had changed slightly. He had initially believed the rapture would be before the tribulation, but he had come to believe the rapture would follow the tribulation. This, he was told, would not be a problem and he would be accepted. Believing this was God's will, Bill and Hetty applied for the one-year mission course in Missouri, USA.

As they drew near to graduation and the end of school, Bill and Hetty were blessed with a son, Mark, but their joy was tempered with the news of the death of Bill's father three days later. Consequently, right after graduation they went home to England for the summer before going on to Missouri for the mission course.

---

[7] See also Payne, "The Reformation Movement Among Baptists in Ontario," 11.

Tested in Missouri

Their three months in Missouri were a time of great testing for Bill and Hetty. From the moment they arrived, they felt they did not fit in, yet they were sure this was God's will for them. To start with, the owner of the place where they lived did not like any noise and their seven-month-old baby naturally made noise. Then again, the church they had to go to was totally different to what they were used to. There was practically no teaching for the Christian. The whole service was geared around the appeal to sinners and the altar call. One Sunday, the altar call lasted 30 to 40 minutes and was so broad: for salvation, re-dedication, baptism, church membership, forgiveness for sins committed that week, etc., so that only a few people, including Bill and Hetty were left in their seats!

When the other students at the Bible school realized Bill knew the different positions of prophecy, they asked if he could give a lecture on them. Bill ended up giving two lectures where he explained all the views to his fellow students. It was interesting because many of the students and even some of the professors had never head the amillennial position explained before. Needless to say, Bill's lectures caused quite a stir among the students. This situation made Bill and Hetty realize how thankful they should be to God for sending them to a school that taught all the views on this topic. However, Bill and Hetty were beginning to get confused: What was God doing in their lives?

On the positive side, the mission course was extremely good. They studied such practical topics as dealing with the missionary's personal life, what was expected of the missionary and how to reach out to different people. But the more they learned of the mission field, the more disturbed they became. Bill was determined to get to the field, though, for he knew too many people who had started out and had never gotten there. That was not going to happen to him. He was so determined it became hard to hear God's voice, but slowly Bill began to understand that what he was being taught about the work on the mission field did not exactly fit with his gifts, which were obviously those of preaching and teaching. Then there was the seemingly never-ending problem of prophecy. If they went with this missionary society, they had to sign a statement of faith, which, of course, involved belief in a pretribulational rapture. Even though they had been assured it would not matter, it obviously did. After much study, reading of books, prayer and desperately trying to find a way to agree with this position, Bill and Hetty decided before God that they could not sign the statement of faith. The mission board met and turned down their application. What a bitter disappointment it was.

What to do next? Where to go? Bill had been so sure this was God's will and now the door was closed. Where was God in all this? Where had they gone wrong? Looking back, they realized God was still there, even though they were confused and felt they had lost their way. God's plans were unfolding; Bill was being forced to consider ministry in a church, which would actually become his life ministry.

Led into the pastorate

Bill decided the best thing they could do at this time was to go back to where they knew they were in God's will. They had no money to get back home to England, so they packed everything they owned in a small U-Haul and travelled back to Toronto, Canada. Bill felt that for a few months he should be "still before God" and see what would unfold. But the mission field was still dear to his heart and he would not contemplate anything other than full-time service for his Lord whom he loved greatly.

TBS gave them a place to stay, where they could keep body and soul together. As it was December, Bill was hired by the Eaton's department store for the Christmas period. After Christmas Bill worked in a factory packing bottles. They moved into a basement apartment and each weekend Bill would try to get a preaching engagement. These were difficult months, as Bill struggled to find what God wanted him to do. Gradually, it seemed that God was leading him into a "pulpit" ministry, so he started to test the water to see if God would open a door. Yet, he was determined that, after two or three years, they would try again to see if the door to the mission field was still closed. Even though Bill never did go to the mission field, he would never lose his burden for the Muslim people.

In July 1964, Bill commenced his ministry at Calvary Baptist Church in Burlington, Ontario. During his eight years there as pastor the church outgrew its building and the congregation decided to step forward in faith and purchase land with a view to building a larger church. Land was secured north of the Queen Elizabeth Way (QEW) highway and a beautiful new building was erected.

At the same time, though, God was taking Bill and Hetty through some deep waters in their personal lives. On October 11, 1965, a son was born,

John Charles, who had Down Syndrome and a serious heart condition. He lived for six months, being very ill for the last three months. This was a very difficult time for Bill, who had to keep up his ministry, while Hetty and baby John were back and forth to the hospital. On looking back, they could see how God used this time in their lives to help them reach others in similar circumstances. God gave them a great love and compassion for the people entrusted to their care. In 1967, to their great joy, a healthy little boy was born, a brother for Mark, named Stephen.

During this time at Calvary, Bill began to read the Puritans and realized the Reformed faith had to encompass *all* areas of life and worship, and not simply be a head knowledge. This meant, among other things, eventually implementing some change in the worship services. Bill was convinced God was directing him in the formation of a Reformed Baptist church based on the doctrines of grace as found in the *Second London Confession of Faith*. These changes were not universally accepted within the congregation and, as resistance came to a head, Bill and Hetty would find themselves moving on to an entirely new work.

2

Setting down roots

The 1970s

◇◇◇◇◇◇◇◇

Speaking to the people of God

Before exploring the history of any church plant, it can be helpful to examine some of the areas seen as essential by the man the Lord uses as chief planter. Much of this is certainly evident in Pastor Payne's preaching and, with copies of sermon notes on file from the beginning of his ministry, an interested and persistent individual could go back and trace the chief currents of thought running through his biblical expositions. However, beginning in February 1969 (the first full year in their new church building), Pastor Payne began issuing regular pastoral letters (usually monthly) to the congregation of Calvary Baptist Church. A selection of comments from these letters reveal elements of his pastoral heart and his willingness to address challenging issues head-on as they applied to his flock:

...in this first letter we must surely press home the need for every member to recognize their personal responsibility to serve the Lord to the best of their ability.[1]

We have spoken frankly, but the issue is too serious to do otherwise. We are not meeting our financial commitments and our work is being hindered through lack of finances. I call on you, my fellow church member, to fully bear your part of the load in this great work. Please do not simply lay this letter aside and forget it. I am asking you to translate it into action from you, personally.[2]

[re: absenteeism during the summer months] How genuine are our convictions? How deep is our Christianity? How seriously do we take our spiritual responsibilities? The summer months often provide revealing answers to these questions. I wonder what impression is left with our children and our neighbours during the summer as regards the importance we place on our church and its ministry.[3]

Some (of our visitors) are Christians and some are not, but whatever their spiritual state, I want to urge you, as a member of the church, to practice these words with respect to them—fellowship, hospitality, and friendship.[4]

If we desire to see His blessing upon our work in 1970, we must be a praying people, not only individually but as a church body. We must pray together; we must gather as a family at the throne united in a common sense of our need, in a common desire for God's glory and a common concern for the souls of men. This is a burden on my heart; I am praying that God will make it one on yours.[5]

If you feel the lack of spiritual freshness in your life just now, let the beauty of spring stir you up. Pray specifically for a fresh touch from God, for a renewed filling of His Spirit. Pray that He would assist you

---

[1] Calgary Baptist Church, pastoral letter, Feb. 1969.
[2] Calgary Baptist Church, pastoral letter, March 1969.
[3] Calgary Baptist Church, pastoral letter, June 1969.
[4] Calgary Baptist Church, pastoral letter, Sept. 1969.
[5] Calgary Baptist Church, pastoral letter, Jan. 1970.

in reinvigorating your prayer life; pray that He would impress His truth deep in your heart. Meditate on the truth of His Word, especially His amazing love, so sovereignly and freely bestowed upon one so unworthy, and may your life and mine have a spiritual freshness about them which will bear the unmistakable message—they have been with Jesus.[6]

Many Christians have become bystanders and spectators and never consider that evangelism is their task at all. But, my Christian friend, evangelism (simply communicating the gospel) is most assuredly your responsibility. It was one of the reasons for the progress of the early church, that every Christian regarded evangelism as their responsibility. It is one of the reasons for our lack of progress today, that few Christians regard it.[7]

If God gave His all for you, can your response be anything less than the total giving of yourself to Him? Paul called Christ God's "unspeakable gift" and, this Christmas season, in the light of that "unspeakable gift" will you hold back any area of your life from the God who loved you so? Must you not, will you not acknowledge that God has the right to all of you? Does not the giving of Christ evoke in you the response of complete love, obedience and service?[8]

God's Word is to instruct us, to teach us. We must study the Bible. We must apply our minds to its teaching to discover what it is saying. To be enriched by the Word and molded by the Word, we must study the Word. It will take time, effort, and concentration, but it is the price of a strong, virile and useful life. I hope that Bible study won't be just an expression to you but a vital part of your life.[9]

Many times we Christians lament loudly when, by a vote of parliament or some other procedure, things go the "wrong way," but most of us are guilty of doing nothing to try to cause them to go the "right way." I

---

[6] Calgary Baptist Church, pastoral letter, Apr. 1970.
[7] Calgary Baptist Church, pastoral letter, Nov. 1970.
[8] Calgary Baptist Church, pastoral letter, Dec. 1970.
[9] Calgary Baptist Church, pastoral letter, May 1971.

confess myself to be as guilty as anyone else in this matter. However, have not things gone far enough to move us as Christians out of our lethargy. Surely Christians ought to be writing letters to newspapers and their MP to make their views known and to call for that righteousness in our land, which alone can "exalt a nation." The advocates of evil are seldom quiet! They have no hesitancy in making their views known. Should not the Christians let it be known that there are still those in Canada concerned about Christian teaching and morality in our society? …Let us speak out in the name of our Lord.[10]

Having given the subject considerable thought, having discussed it with other evangelical pastors and reading and listening to the views of various doctors, I feel strongly that Christian people ought to oppose the "abortion on demand" position. Of all people, Christians ought to value human life, believing, as we do, that it is the gift of God. …Our society has enough to answer for before the bar of God's justice. Let us do all we can as Christians to prevent further degradation.[11]

This brief selection of exhortations, clarifications and challenges to his congregation may help provide a greater appreciation for the things that weighed most on Pastor Payne's heart and mind as he sought to give sound pastoral leadership to his people. This, combined with an understanding of how strongly he held to the biblical doctrines of sovereign grace, reveals something of the spiritual core of the man used by God to found Trinity Baptist Church.

First steps

The Lord has often used upheaval and conflict before He brings about healing and then builds anew. This was the experience of Pastor Payne and his family in the early 1970s. He had begun pastoral work at Calvary Baptist Church, Burlington, in July 1964 but, as the 60s ended and the 70s began, it became increasingly apparent that the substance of the teaching and preaching that had become central to Pastor Payne's ministry, based on his understanding of Scripture, was no longer welcome or appreciated.

---

[10] Calgary Baptist Church, pastoral letter, Oct. 1971.
[11] Calgary Baptist Church, pastoral letter, Jan. 1972.

This lack of enthusiasm became evident through meetings and conversations with certain members of the board and the wider congregation. As a result, a congregational vote was held on the future of his ministry at Calvary. The night of the vote, June 14, 1972, Pastor Payne had the opportunity to speak to the membership and he addressed the concerns raised by some members regarding *"dissatisfaction with the ministry of the pastor and [a warning] that they will terminate membership if things continue as they are."* In a final appeal to the church membership, Pastor Payne sought to clarify his position on several issues and, at the heart of his defense, offered the following:

> As we come together to vote tonight, I believe in my heart that this church is at the crossroads. It has to choose whether to stand for the truth of God and the preaching of the whole counsel of God or stand in rejection of a large part of that truth. It needs to be clear in the mind of every member that the pastor is not on trial; it is the church that is on trial! There is a basic and very serious malady here, evidencing itself in elements of new-evangelism, coupled with a superficiality in the things of the Spirit....It is obvious that a man and his ministry go together. You must have believed that it was God's will for me to come here [note: the earlier vote to bring him on as pastor had been unanimous, even after clearly stating his position on the doctrines on which he was now being challenged], yet you do not seem to have faith enough to perceive that it may be His will that we be led into deeper and more God-glorifying truths, before going on to do great things in His Name.

Thus, even to the end, he maintained a loving, pastoral concern for the souls of those in his charge. However, the church vote was held and, after the result was tallied, it became clear the desire of the membership was divided, with the majority looking for new pastoral leadership. To avoid a second vote and potential split, the board expressed the feeling that the pastor should resign, which he did on June 25. In a final statement to the membership he concluded:

> It seems that the underlying concern of a great majority of the members is to hold together a compromising situation that is dishonouring to the Lord. I as a preacher, called of God to maintain and

proclaim God's truth, and defend His honour, can have no part in this, and therefore I have no option but to resign as pastor.

Saddened, but not broken at the news, he and his family laid themselves in the hands of the Lord and looked to Him for direction and strength. Almost immediately, he was approached by several people from Calvary who expressed agreement with his view of Scripture and demonstrated a corporate desire to establish a new "Reformed Baptist" work; they agreed in general to explore the feasibility of making a fresh start.

This group had a strong desire to move ahead as soon as possible. Like many groups before them, this one began small enough to meet in a person's home; in this case it was that of John and Wilma Haughie at 733 Ashley Avenue in Burlington. The first meeting was held on Sunday October 8, 1972, where the seed of a church met for both morning and evening services. At that first gathering, Pastor Payne preached on Psalm 48:14, seeking to encourage the people with the unfailing faithfulness of God as their guide.

> Now I find it a very precious thought this morning that God is concerned about His church. That's the kind of God that He is; this is the prime reason why we are here this morning, because we are concerned about the church of God and the only reason that concern is in our hearts is because that concern is in God's heart.

In his conclusion, as he exhorted the people to look ahead in faith, he stated,

> This God knows the way infallibly, He knows all the dangers, all the problem areas and He knows the end from the beginning. When this God takes a people in hand and deigns to be their guide they may have confidence that He will bring them to that place which both they and He desire.

Their first look was to God their Father and, by His grace, that look remained fixed on Him.

To go from a body of interested believers to a fully functioning church, numerous plans needed to be explored and many decisions made—everyone agreed the sooner this was done the better! So, that very week, on

Wednesday, October 11, the group met again at the Haughies and, among other things, decided on the following:

1. Marjorie Pearce was appointed temporary secretary, to keep minutes of meetings.
2. A Reformed Baptist Church was to be established and named *Trinity Baptist Church*.
3. An Interim Constitution was presented and accepted.
4. The Reverend William E. Payne was called to accept the position of pastor.
5. Trefoil Lodge was to be the official place for meeting.
6. A five-man finance committee was appointed until deacons and elders could be established (Dr. Colin Wellum, Mr. Don Leggatt, Mr. Bob Laing, Mr. Dale Clarke and Mr. Hugh Clarke as Treasurer)
7. In addition to meeting on Sunday, there would be a prayer meeting held Wednesday evening.

Because the Lord had laid this common vision for a new work on the hearts of several families, there were plenty of willing workers. Spiritual and practical gifts were soon identified and those in attendance quickly coalesced and became a congregation, a church family. In very short order, Trinity Baptist Church was born; the first official services were held the following Sunday, October 15, 1972, at Trefoil Lodge, a Girl Guide meeting place, on Brant St. just north of Caroline St.

In his inaugural message, Pastor Payne clearly laid out his vision for the church. He made it very clear he was excited about the church being both *Baptistic* and *Reformed*.

> If I were to be asked "What kind of a church are you?" I would not hesitate to reply, "We are a Baptist church!" We hold to those truths which have sometimes been referred to as "Baptist Distinctives." I would also reply that we are a "Reformed Church" inasmuch as we hold to the great doctrines of the Reformation in the areas concerning the salvation of men. In this sense, I am not at all averse to our church being referred to as a "Reformed Baptist" church.

He then went on to focus on the centrality of Scripture as a guide to Christian living, the necessity of preaching and teaching the whole counsel of God, understanding and embracing the doctrines of grace, the absolute need for evangelism and the argument for reverent congregational worship. No one who heard the first sermon to that newly formed congregation could have any doubts as to where their pastor stood in all these essential areas.

Over the first few months, congregational business meetings were held on a regular basis. There were many decisions to be made and the leadership wanted all things to be done decently and in order. For example, at a meeting on October 25, 1972, the church family decided on a salary of $775 per month for the pastor, with some additional funds set aside for local advertising. They prayed specifically for the government to move quickly on their application for registration which, in fact, arrived on November 7, reminding us that some issues were handled more speedily in the pre-tech days. Ushers were appointed and regular church offerings were taken starting Sunday, November 13. Knowing the importance of ministry to the children, they rented a local public school facility on Wednesday evenings and established Family Night, beginning November 15, where, from 7:00 to 8:30 p.m., separate programs were offered to all age groups, with the remaining adults meeting for prayer. God was merciful in laying the desire for a new work on the hearts of so many people. Though not many mighty and noble were in attendance, the Lord used the plain people of the world, equipped and enabled by His Spirit, to see this work established on a firm foundation of scriptural truth and Christian love.

Trefoil Lodge, though a wonderful first stop for the church, had limitations on space which prevented the creation of an adequate nursery and offered no provision for Sunday School classes. Consequently, the cheerful sounds that arise naturally from a nursery could not be kept from the folks in the service sitting on the other side of the very thin door that separated the kitchen and the main hall. As well, with the congregation already totalling nearly 65, the Lodge was visibly shrinking in its suitability. At their November 8th meeting various alternatives were raised and discussed, and, since the obtaining of a church building did not seem feasible at the time, the most hopeful option was to seek out a public school to use temporarily. This resulted in a move to Central Public School on Brant St. beginning February 4, 1973. This new facility would allow for the worship services to be held in the school auditorium with various classrooms providing sufficient space for the beginning of a much-needed Sunday School program.

Pastor Payne took every opportunity to teach and reveal the deep truths found in every part of Scripture, particularly the great doctrines of sovereign grace, doctrines he had come to love and embrace over the previous number of years. When the first church bulletin was printed in December 1972 (they came out monthly in the early years), he offered these thoughts in a section entitled, "From the Pastor's Desk":

> One of the prime reasons for our existence as a church is our desire to give witness to those precious truths of the Scriptures which we, for summation, call THE DOCTRINES OF GRACE. Being revealed and highly exalted by the Lord, they are very precious to us.
>
> It is interesting and instructive to note as Christmas comes upon us once again that God gave witness to these doctrines in the "Christmas announcement" of Matt. 1:21: "Thou shalt call His name Jesus, for He shall save His people from their SINS." The "sins" from which people must be delivered are a reality because of the "sin" which corrupts human nature. A right understanding of "sin" will convince us of the truth of the doctrine of "total depravity."
>
> "He shall save HIS PEOPLE"...God has a people; a people chosen by divine grace from before the foundation of the world. Surely this is the doctrine of "election."
>
> "He shall SAVE"...How did Jesus save? He did it by standing in the room and stead of sinners, bearing their sins in His own body and offering Himself to God as the propitiation for sins. Here is the atonement by Christ. But the angel declared, "He shall SAVE His PEOPLE": here is a "definite and particular atonement."
>
> "He SHALL save"...It is not that He shall attempt to or He desires to, but He SHALL save them! Here is the doctrine of "effectual calling" or "irresistible grace," assuring us that the Lord Jesus Christ shall not be disappointed, but that He shall indeed bring ALL His sheep into the fold.
>
> "HE shall save His people"...Here we are reminded that salvation is indeed the work of God, and it is just because that is true that God's people shall persevere to the end by His grace. This is SECURITY made by the Lord!
>
> So, in that beautiful announcement of the angel to Joseph we have, in essence, ALL those glorious doctrines so precious to our hearts and so honouring to God.[12]

---

[12] Trinity Baptist Church, Bulletin, Dec. 1972.

"From the Pastor's Desk" was to become a regular feature of those early church bulletins, where the pastor examined a wide range of topics including family issues, finances, the Lord's Day, the reality of the devil, even how to combat the "worldly tinsel avalanche" at Christmas. His goal was to shepherd the people by offering wisdom and teaching related to the struggles faced by believers every day.

Steps to greater formality

With the dawn of 1973, the church moved to implement several aspects of the newly minted church constitution. These early decisions were made by the official founding membership which totalled 32 people:

Founding membership

Audrey Brouwers	Mrs. R. Duez	Marjorie Pearce
Mrs. J. Brouwers	Mr. R. Duez	Barbara Redman
Mr. J. Brouwers	Mrs. J. Haughie	Mrs. R. Schaub
Mrs. Jan Brouwers	Mr. J. Haughie	Mr. R. Schaub
Mr. Jan Brouwers	Brian Haughie	Mrs. C. Wellum
Mrs. H. Clarke	Mr. B. Langford	Dr. C. Wellum
Mr. H. Clarke	Mrs. D. Leggett	Mrs. R. Wilkins
Mrs. R. Clarke	Mr. D. Leggett	Mr. R. Wilkins
Mr. R. Clarke	Pat McMahon	Mrs. D. Wilson
Steven Clarke	Mrs. Wm. Payne	Mr. D. Wilson
Russell Clarke	Rev. Wm. Payne	

One of the early priorities was to elect the first church officers, namely elders and deacons. Pastor Payne took time to instruct the congregation on the biblical qualifications and functions for both offices. Then, meeting on January 5th, once again at the Haughie's home, the first elders and deacons were appointed. Ideally, each man should serve a four-year term then take a mandatory year off. However, in this instance, to avoid having the four-year term of all the officers end at the same time, men were appointed for either a 1, 2, 3 or 4-year term. The following men came on as elders: Hugh Clarke—4 years, John Haughie—3 years, Bob Wilkins—2 years, Roy Schaub—1 year. The first church deacons were also appointed based on similar reasoning: Jack Brouwers—3 years, Bob Clarke—2 years, Dale Wilson—1 year. A biblical framework of leadership was now in place to guide the church family going forward.

With the move from Trefoil Lodge to Central Public School, the much larger facility allowed for worship services in the school auditorium and Sunday School in the various classrooms, another direct answer to prayer. By the end of that month there were, including the teachers, over 60 in attendance spread over 7 age groups, with about 45 from nursery to the teen class. The first wave of teachers included Mrs. Hetty Payne, Dr. Colin Wellum and his wife Joan, members the Lord would continue to use in ministry for decades to come!

Over the next few months, foundational issues related to regular church life occupied the members. The first financial statement was presented and showed a total income of about $2,500; this was used as the basis for the first church budget. With an eye to the future, a committee was established to search for a possible church home: either to purchase an existing building or find a suitable property on which a church could be built. Practical matters were not to be overlooked and the church approved four weeks of annual vacation for the pastor, something that would be greatly appreciated by the entire Payne family over the years. Only a pastor's family can really understand the daily personal cost of leading a church plant. On April 15, Bob and Jean Laing were the first individuals to be baptized and join the church; Emmanuel Baptist Church in Milton graciously offered the use of their facility for this event. The church family was blessed by the contribution of teachers other than Pastor Payne in these early days. Rev. Bob Duez offered a day of teaching to "Focus on the Family" and John Reisinger spoke on "Salvation by the Sovereign Grace of God" during a four-evening series set up as an evangelical outreach. In June, the church agreed to support their first missionaries, Hugh and Jean Gordon, who were working in Pakistan. With John Haughie stepping down as elder for health reasons, Dr. Colin Wellum was appointed to take his place, a position Dr. Wellum would hold for almost 40 years! At the same time Jean Laing became the official church secretary, a position she would hold for over 40 years! It is doubtful if any members anticipated such a long period of service in those early days, but the stability offered by faithful, long-term service was a blessing to the new work. The church family was also growing via individual family growth as Trinity's first baby, Cynthia Leigh Van Zanden, was born on October 11th; many more were to follow.[13]

---

[13] See Appendix 7.

At the first annual business meeting in October, the church members dug down financially and committed to offering the pastor an 8% raise and set his salary at $10,080! Among the key items for discussion, apart from the budget, included: (i) Trinity Christian School on Walkers Line being considered as a new church home; (ii) reducing the number of members meetings and facilitating the duties of the board by authorizing them to spend up to $500 without going to the membership; and (iii) a 2/3 majority vote by eligible members would now be required for the appointment of church officers. Step by step, the organizational framework of an ordered church was being established.

This brings the church to the close of its first full year. Much had been accomplished. Sadly, some families or individuals had, for a variety of reasons, already moved on, but new families had also joined. The first anniversary was celebrated with much thanksgiving to God for His kindness and faithfulness toward them as a congregation. Appropriately, Pastor Payne preached the first anniversary message, though in future years a special speaker would be invited to take this service. These speakers would come from all over the world,[14] but each one would help the congregation rejoice with a life-changing message from the ever applicable, beautiful Word of God.

Early areas of emphasis

It would be impractical to try and record all the details of the life of a church. Perhaps it would be enlightening, however, to identify some of the areas of greatest emphasis that emerged as Trinity developed in those first few years.

Central purpose and focus

In Pastor Payne's outline of their early priorities, he stated the following in a tenth anniversary article about Trinity in *The Gospel Witness*:

> The church was committed to certain fundamental principles, among them the primacy of the preaching of the Word of God; the declaration of the great doctrines of grace as witnessed to in the historic *Baptist Confession of Faith of 1689*; biblical evangelism; and

---

[14] See Appendix 6.

the uniting of reverence with joy in the service. A church motto was selected based on the words of Paul in Acts 20:27—"declaring all the counsel of God."[15]

At times, pressures would sweep through from the evangelical world that sought to move the church away from these foundational moorings and align it with lesser things. The Lord was gracious in enabling the church to maintain its reliability on the clear teachings found in the Word. Pastor Payne was an excellent spiritual sailor and helped guide the congregation through potentially rough waters to safer harbours.

Prayer

There has never been any doubt at Trinity that Scripture sets prayer near the pinnacle of Christian privilege and responsibility. Coming to the throne of grace with praise, petition and thanksgiving lifts a believer's soul to the highest of heights and helps develop and maintain a close, personal walk with the Lord. The need for regular, fervent and specific private and corporate intercession must always be the spiritual lifeblood of any serious-minded congregation. In terms of corporate prayer, the mid-week prayer meeting has been at the heart of Trinity's ministry from the very first week. Pastor Payne often referred to the necessity of meeting to pray:

> These are days when the spiritual conflict is intense and Christians who are wise will take every opportunity to be strengthened and encouraged in the things of God. Christians who are not only wise but concerned will also take every opportunity to strengthen and encourage one another, and also seek God's face earnestly for His power and blessing on His church. Remember, that to the question, "Where is the God of Elijah?" the answer comes back, "Where are the Elijahs of God?"[16]

Meeting the needs of the kids

The local church should certainly be a source of evangelical outreach to the lost. The way of salvation and the desperate need to pursue it in Christ forms an aspect of every well thought out message. However, the local church has an even greater responsibility for the spiritual welfare of her

---

[15] *The Gospel Witness*, Dec. 30, 1982.
[16] *The Gospel Witness*, Dec. 30, 1982.

members and adherents. Church congregations are largely made up of families which are, in turn, largely made up of children. Trinity's children, and those in the local neighbourhood, were of great importance to the men on the board, especially to Pastor Payne. Even though young children were expected to take part in the regular church services (nursery ended when a child turned 3), the importance of having age-appropriate programs was always a priority. Sunday School and the Wednesday evening programs offered teaching and topics aimed at specific age groups. These activities and efforts were supported by consistent prayer for the spiritual transformation and salvation of the children.

As part of this focus, children were often highlighted in brief news items in the bulletin, intended to encourage children and young people to take advantage of the opportunities for fun, fellowship and study offered through church programs. For example, the March 1974 bulletin included 10 pages of pictures, quotes and brief personal profiles covering all the youth in the church. One obvious goal was to increase awareness and prayer from the members for these young people. At times, the youth were invited to submit drawings on a given theme (Easter for example) and some would be chosen to appear in the bulletin on an appropriate date. There were simplified teachings offered to instruct children in behaviour that pleased God and did good to others. For example, in a July 1977 bulletin there were "Six Short Rules for Young Christians" by Brownlow North. Number 3 on that list:

> Never let a day pass without trying to do something for Jesus. Every night reflect on what Jesus has done for you and then ask yourself, "What am I doing for Him?"

Reference was then made to Matthew 5:13–16 to help the children and their parents see the biblical support for such an attitude.

One of the great outside attractions for younger boys and girls in those days were the programs offered through the Boy Scouts and Girl Guides. To provide activity-based programs built on more spiritual foundations, a Pioneer Girls program was begun along with Trinity Boy's Club, held on Tuesday evenings. At these meetings the children sang songs, played games, created numerous arts and crafts to adorn their family homes and learned the critical need of becoming a follower of Jesus and the nature and value of a sound Christian character. They were then encouraged to reflect on how they could better serve the Lord, even in their younger years, usually by serving others in the Lord's name. There were times these children participated in regular church services, usually presented as a special Youth Service. They would greet people at the door, read Scripture, collect the offering and provide some special music. In those early days, the leadership believed young people needed to see they were an essential and valued component of the congregation. Their participation was a source of real joy to everyone.

Reading good books

The congregation was certainly encouraged not only to read their Bibles daily, but, by prayer, meditation and study, seek to grasp as much of its immeasurable wealth as possible. One way to help this process was to read good Christian literature, written by those who have proved they can handle the Word well. Pastor Payne was widely read, especially in the world of the Reformers and Puritans and those who were like-minded. Whether through subtle or not-so-subtle means, he created a consistent undercurrent that told the congregation there was always something good out there they should read for their own spiritual benefit. For years, most bulletins contained some reference, usually a quote, from a bygone day whose message was still perfectly applicable to the present. Over time the congregation encountered quotes from: J.C. Ryle, Horatius Bonar, David Brainerd, Charles Spurgeon (he was perhaps Pastor Payne's favourite!), Henry Mahan, A.W. Pink, Octavius Winslow, John Murray, Thomas Boston, Thomas Watson, John Owen, H.C.G Moule, Robert Traill, John Flavel, Martin Luther, J.R. Caldwell, R. Govett, Thomas Brooks, Samuel Rutherford, Iain Murray, Dr. Martyn Lloyd Jones and others! These, all on their own, would make a reading list sufficient for a lifetime. To facilitate access to this kind of literature, a book table was set out in the summer of 1974 and, in the fall, a portable library was set up and overseen by Hugh Clarke.

Pastor Payne was an admirer of pithy sayings, especially those attributed to the Reformers, Puritans and later writers who seemed to have a grasp on the English language that rivalled Shakespeare and other literary greats. He was not simply impressed with the concise aspect of the language used, but more so for the scriptural truth it helped lock into the brain:

"The best of men are men at best."[17]

---

[17] Circa 1680; possibly John Flavel.

"Either this book [the Bible] will keep you from sin or sin will keep you from this book."[18]

"Sin forsaken is one of the best evidences of sins forgiven."[19]

He also urged the people to read Christian biographies as a means of encouragement. God often used very ordinary people in extraordinary ways. It was also important to understand that even the "greats" battled many of the same fears, frustrations and failures that members of the congregation encountered, yet they remained faithful to God and God to them. In his messages and writings, there would be regular references to publications such as: *The Sword and Trowel* (edited by John Reisinger), the *1689 Baptist Confession of Faith*, *Children's Catechism*, the *Gospel Clarion*, *Quarterly Reports of the Trinitarian Bible Society*, *Reformation Today*, *The Seminarian* and *Spurgeon's Sermons* (a distribution ministry of sermons begun at Blair Baptist Church and eventually taken up by Bath Road Baptist Church in Kingston).

At times, he would include snatches of hymns from published writers and composers as well as the writings of a more local nature, written by members of the congregation. He himself wrote over a hundred hymns in his lifetime, though most of them remained out of public view until after his death. There are now over fifty of them available to be sung in *Trinity Praise*, a supplement to Trinity's hymnal.

Missions

Earlier in their married life, Pastor Payne and his wife Hetty had felt the Lord's call to missions, and to the Muslim world in particular. As time unfolded, however, God showed them this was not the path for them to take and He led them into pastoral work. Nonetheless, their passion for missions never subsided. Soon after Trinity was founded, they took up the challenge and privilege of helping to get individuals to the mission field and provide ongoing support.

In his May 1972 letter to the congregation at Calvary Baptist Church (just prior to stepping down), Pastor Payne made this urgent appeal for a special offering aimed at helping missionaries in great financial need:

---

[18] Written inside the cover of John Bunyan's Bible.
[19] J.C. Ryle.

Our aim is for $1,000; we need you to at least double your regular offering. Is that really a lot to ask in the light of the need and in the light of our Saviour's sacrifice for us? Let us make a concerted effort; give, even if it hurts—and keep giving. If necessary, deprive yourself of some item on which you would usually spend money. But, for the glory of God, for the sake of dying souls and out of love for the One who gave so much for us, let us put a great offering at His feet for His disposal.

In June 1973, Hugh and Jean Gordon, serving in Pakistan with International Christian Fellowship, were taken on as the first missionaries to be supported by Trinity Baptist Church. The support was $10 per month. Not long after, a young couple connected to Wycliffe Bible Translators in the Philippines, Peter and Chris Green, were added to the missions roster. Within the next two years, the Pioneer Girls had helped support Joan Brown in Ethiopia and the church voted to support Terry and Gail Tiessen at the Asian Theological Seminary in the Philippines. Though modest at the outset, the need to support and send missionaries to fulfill the great commission of Jesus Christ to go into all the world was planted deep in the hearts and minds of the congregation and they have faithfully been mission minded ever since! Trinity is thankful for the leadership, especially in those formative years, that led the church into a sacrificial appreciation for the work, and the workers, far afield.

Neighbourhood connections
A month of Tuesday evenings were set aside in May 1974, to distribute books and literature to some of the neighbouring homes. In addition, visitation to nearby families was planned and carried out in September. At the time, it wasn't strange to have a person show up on your doorstep with an interest in sharing the gospel, though the practice has fallen more and more out of favour. Trinity was no "secretive group." They tried to broadcast their message as much as possible to those living nearby. Ads in the local newspapers (Milton and Burlington) were utilized to announce regular weekly services, as well as special meetings throughout the year, including the weekly meetings for kids. It was apparent there could be greater success in these ventures once the church had its own building that, once firmly established, would be recognizable to everyone in the area.

Singing

In Pastor Payne's letter to the church in November 1972, he identified what the appropriate attitude of the church family should be toward singing. His position was made crystal clear as he spoke joyfully about their newly arrived hymnbooks:

> We were glad when our hymnbooks arrived, and many have already come to really appreciate them. They have made a definite contribution to our services. May our church soon become renowned for great congregational singing of glorious hymns! Admittedly, it would be been nice to have a book with music in; but when the choice is between a hymnbook with solid and glorious hymns of the faith, so meaningful and relevant to every aspect of Christian life, doctrine and thought, and a hymnbook with music but with second rate content, then the choice must surely be the former. Thank God for the great hymns which we have in our book; let us learn them and sing them with fervour to the glory of God.

Singing has always been a significant part of every Trinity worship service. Pastor Payne had an excellent voice and led by fervent and energetic example. He challenged the congregation to learn new hymns on a regular basis, while still holding to favourites adopted along the way. In 1976, he was excited to recommend a new hymnbook to the congregation, *Grace Hymns*, which continued to live at the heart of hymnody at Trinity for many years.

In May 1979, he offered an interesting observation by Spurgeon regarding singing:

> We should do well if we added to our godly service more singing. The world sings: the million have their songs; and I must say that the taste of the populace is a very remarkable taste just now as to its favourite songs. They are, many of them, so absurd and meaningless as to be unworthy of an idiot. I should insult an idiot if I could suppose that such songs as people sing nowadays would really be agreeable to him. Yet, these things will be heard from men and places will be thronged to hear the stuff. Now, why should we, with the grand Psalms we have of David, with the noble hymns of Cowper, Milton and Watts—why should we not sing as well as they? Let us sing the

songs of Zion; they are as cheerful as the songs of Sodom any day. Let us drown the howling nonsense of Gomorrah with the melodies of the New Jerusalem.[20]

Though there would never be universal agreement on where to find the line between true singing and the mere making of a joyful noise, the push for the congregation to find joy in singing songs and hymns of substance was established early on. This is not to say that there was not room for some levity in the right place, as the kids could attest. They sang "Old Lady Leary," "The Austrian Went Yodeling" and" I Met a Bear" at Kids Club with the most exuberant gusto imaginable.

Fellowship for Reformed and Pastoral Studies (FRPS)

In January 1974, a group of pastors began holding a series of monthly meetings. The group was officially titled, FRPS but became better known as "Frips." It was the first of its kind in Canada, as being a Reformed Baptist at that time was considered to be as spiritually "out in left field" as you could get by the larger evangelical world. Pastor Payne was viewed as the visionary in its establishment and early growth. The rationale given for its purpose was outlined by the initial leadership group:

> The initials F.R.P.S. stand for Fellowship for Reformation and Pastoral Studies. It might be expressed simply as a ministers fraternal; an opportunity for pastors to meet on a regular basis (monthly) to hear someone deliver a paper on an assigned topic, and then to enjoy discussion, prayer and fellowship. The FRPS…has proven a most helpful and profitable group for pastors and for students and other friends who are occasionally able to gather. The FRPS was begun by Pastor Leigh Powell (Covenant Baptist Church, Toronto), Pastor Gordon Rumford (Kenmuir Baptist Church, Port Credit), Pastor Roger Fellows (Bowmanville Baptist Church) and Pastor William Payne (Trinity Baptist Church, Burlington). These four men formed the executive of the group.
>
> Papers covering a wide variety of topics have been presented—for example, "The Biblical Teaching on Revival," "The After-Life,"

---

[20] *Flashes of Thought: 1000 Choice Extracts, From the Works of C.H. Spurgeon* (London: Passmore & Alabaster, 1874), #792.

"John Knox—An Anniversary Tribute," "The Biblical Purpose for Tongues," "The Centrality of Scripture" and "Limited Atonement—its Implications for Evangelism." As opportunity arises, special guests are invited to present papers to the group and Rev. Herbert Carson and Rev. Erroll Hulse have both participated in recent months. Some time ago Rev. Stanford Reid of the Univ. of Guelph gave a fascinating paper on "The Reformation in Old and New France."

The FRPS hopes to encourage projects which will encourage a return to the doctrines of grace and strong biblical preaching among the churches of Canada. At this moment, a Bible conference is being arranged for the month of May, to be held at Royal York Road Baptist Church and other projects are being considered. We bring the FRPS to the attention of our members and friends so that you will be aware of its ministry and so that you pray for its work.[21]

This pastoral ministry, as envisioned by its founders, has been blessed by the Lord over the years and, through the hundreds of papers presented, has fulfilled its original intent. It was rebranded as TPF (Toronto Pastor's Fellowship) for a while and eventually became the GPF (Grace Pastor's Fellowship). It continues to offer a welcome platform for teaching, discussion, fellowship and prayerful intercession.[22] Reformation is always necessary when the eyes of believers are tempted to digress from the core, essential truths of the gospel. Trinity's overlapping ministry with FRPS became an integral part of her church planting program.

Accountability

There was always a desire to keep things within the church as transparent as possible. There were regular business meetings set up to discuss proposals, hammer out details and pray for the Lord's strength and direction at every step. Financial details were always made available to members of the congregation. As well, so people could be fully aware of how things were progressing in all areas of church work, annual departmental reports began to be presented in Fall 1975. This was an informative and beneficial practice that continues to the present day.

---

[21] Trinity Baptist Church, Bulletin, Feb. 1975.
[22] For more information, see https://www.sgfcanada.com/gpf.

The church constitution was written in a way that allowed members to clearly understand how church practice should unfold, offering biblical support wherever necessary. For example, steps were clearly delineated for the process of nominating and voting for church officers, including the pastor. Timelines were established that allowed members the opportunity to consider big decisions that, if not handled openly and carefully, held the potential to harm the church and dishonour the Lord. There were checks and balances to properly oversee issues such as church discipline, membership and finances. All members were exhorted to participate in the decision-making process: they were part of the body of Christ and had a responsibility to see that this local body acted in a way that would please God and promote sound worship, good order and strong church unity.

The church body entrusted most of the decisions related to the day to day working of the church to the elders and deacons who comprised the church board. Any proposed change in policy, large financial expenditure, adoption of a mission project or other significant plans were always presented to the members for their consideration, feedback and final decision. It was essential that a high level of trust be established and maintained between the people and the board; this could only be accomplished through open dialogue and consistent faithfulness among all segments of the church body.

Encouragement

With so many people offering their time and talents to the work, it would be easy to overlook those efforts and simply presume on people's willingness to help. Into his comments and notices in the bulletin, the pastor would interject little notes to let the congregation know this was not the case.

> A word of appreciation to our nursery staff. The Nursery has been bursting at the seams at times recently—a fact which makes us very happy—but we know that the work of the Nursery is demanding, and we want the ladies who staff it to know that we appreciate their labours.

As important as it is to serve one another, it is right and biblical to offer thanksgiving to those serving. This is not the reason for serving, but one of the blessings arising from it. Those who served in more public ways would more easily be recognized and appreciated. However, those whose service was less visible would also receive timely and meaningful praise and recognition, especially from the pastor. Members stepped up to serve in many ministries, such as teaching Sunday School, leading Kids Club and Youth Group, maintaining the library, recording services (tape and video), cleaning, playing piano and organ for services, church secretary, church treasurer, envelope steward, missions secretary, ladies fellowship and Bible study, social committee, ushering, the weekly bulletin and even fire marshall. There was something to do for everyone who wished to be involved. It was not a time to simply sit back and be served. It was a time to follow the example of the Lord Jesus and be busy washing one another's feet.

The path to Zimmerman

From the outset, the leadership spoke of the desirability of establishing a permanent home for Trinity Baptist Church. In March 1973, the board appointed a three-person committee to explore the possible purchase of property for a future building or a building itself. In the meantime, at the October 1973 business meeting, a proposal to shift location to Trinity Christian School in Burlington was discussed. This move would alleviate some space concerns and allow for all church ministries, including midweek, to be held at the same facility, simplifying logistics and travel for the congregation. This move would make their presence more stable and predictable for those in the area who showed interest in the church ministries. Certain details made renting an ongoing facility a challenge: the weekly set-up/take-down procedure along with the movement of hymnbooks and nursery supplies in and out of the facility. The decision to change rental locations, however, was made quickly, and the congregation moved in December—Trinity became the new home for Trinity! The church was to meet there for just over two years. During this time, the conviction that a permanent facility was needed, owned and operated solely for the work of the Lord, was growing in intensity and became a focal point of discussion at church meetings.

Because of the existing financial and real estate limitations faced by the church (land was very expensive in Burlington and the surrounding area, and very few suitable church buildings came up for sale), a suggestion was made at the annual business meeting in October 1974, that the church should anticipate remaining where they were for up to three or four years. This was to allow the congregation to grow in number and fortify a building fund above and beyond the church budget, which was set at $18,350 for the upcoming year. The Lord, however, had a different timeframe in mind and the next big move was to get underway much sooner.

Early in 1975, Hugh Clarke drew the attention of the congregation to the fact that the Zimmerman United Church building on Appleby Line at No. 2 Sideroad stood vacant and might be for sale. It had remained virtually unused since 1970, the year the Zimmerman congregation amalgamated with Lowville United Church, vacating the building. There was renewed prayer at that point for the Lord's leading in this matter and, in February 1975, the congregation began serious discussions on the purchase of a church building (possibly Zimmerman United) or a property where a church could be built. The members gave the board permission to examine potential properties up to a value of $50,000. A couple of possibilities emerged: 10 acres at the corner of Appleby Line and No. 1 Sideroad for $53,000 or renting or purchasing Zimmerman United Church. The drive out to these country locations should not be problematic, especially considering the high cost of land closer to the city centre. The option of Zimmerman seemed the most hopeful and so, in April, a meeting was held between representatives from Trinity and Zimmerman to discuss the timing and financial realities of a possible purchase. How significant the gap between asking price and what the church felt it could afford was uppermost in everyone's mind.

At the May business meeting, the congregation made it official: a strong majority voted to pursue the purchase of Zimmerman United, whose appraised value was between $40,000 and $50,000. Trinity was in a position to offer a down payment of $20,000 and approved a maximum offer of purchase of $40,000, but only after an estimate was made on the potential cost of renovations. In June, after the cost estimate was presented, the members authorized a final purchase offer of $30,000 with an additional $50,000 targetted for renovations and upgrades. In the kind providence of God, this offer of purchase was accepted by the people representing Zimmerman and the building and land soon became the property of Trinity Baptist Church. As the pastor indicated in his letter to the membership on June 10, 1975, "This is surely one of those situations where we are constrained to say that God has done 'exceeding abundantly above all that we could ask or think.'"[23]

After a church meeting on June 19, where three options for building renovation were presented to the membership, the decision was made

---

[23] See Ephesians 3:20.

to pursue the plan that provided the maximum amount of floor space at the time. The work was to be overseen by Hank Vander Meullen, a local contractor. He met with church members on June 25th, and on June 29th they accepted his recommendations for construction budgetted at about $58,400. This first addition (27 x 43 feet) was originally planned to be added to the southwest side of the existing 1890 building. Due to its closeness to the edge of the ravine, however, it had to be switched to the north side. This required a variance from the city, which also allowed for the installation of the church's first septic bed. To accommodate this, the yard north of the building was backfilled and a raised septic bed was built on the slope leading down to the northeast. After final renovations, the main auditorium would seat about 140 people, all in the original, wooden, bucket-style, individual seats that flipped up none too quietly!

With a total of $23,000 presently in the building fund, the church was given the challenge of coming up with the other $7,000, so it could be purchased outright. One of the exhortations that came from the pen of Pastor Payne is recorded in "From the Pastor's Desk" in July 1975:

> Though the building is old, it is solidly built and is in very fine condition, the auditorium having been kept in particularly good and attractive condition. Our congregation has approached the purchase of this building with caution, recognizing that there were negative aspects to be considered over against the positive ones, but one of the most encouraging aspects has been that earnest and continual prayer has been made before the Lord for His will to be made apparent, and for His guidance to be granted to us.
>
> However, I think that it is true to say that it has become the growing conviction of the great majority of the membership that this building was indeed the Lord's provision....the fact that our first offer of purchase was accepted, in spite of the fact that it was considerably below the "'asking price," was, for many, the final seal that this matter was indeed of the Lord. As most are aware, we intend to renovate the old building and to add to it.
>
> The most important thing now...is that we should pull together as a congregation and that we should all give ourselves 100% to the testimony to which God has called us. We should pray also that He might grant to us a great spirit of unity and oneness and that His presence might be a reality in these days.

The congregation, moved by the Lord's hand in this whole affair, as well as by this plea from the pastor, responded in a beautifully generous fashion. Don Wheaton described the spirit of the people in an excerpt from the bulletin:

> *July 6th—An Historic Day!* It was the first opportunity for the people in Trinity to face a sizeable financial challenge in order to have enough money on hand to purchase outright Zimmerman United Church. Though the appeal was announced by Dr. Colin Wellum as an "open-ended financial drive" to cover about three Sundays, the people, with small and large gifts, decided to give generously on the first day. There was a spirit of sheer joy in giving to the Lord. Consequently, over 77% (about $5,400) of the goal was reached on the first Sunday [morning]. With the announcement of the total monies realized by the evening service, the people sang as their closing hymn the traditional "Doxology" with deep emotion and profound thanksgiving to the Lord.[24]

In short, the immediate goal of $7,000 was met and exceeded, as the Lord enabled and encouraged His people to give $8,000 in a single day of giving, and to do so with a joyful and cheerful spirit! As a result, the building was purchased without debt; any future borrowed money would be dedicated to the planned renovation and extension work. Once again the Lord showed Himself faithful to the needs of His people.

There was a lot of work to be done to the building before the congregation could move in. The new addition to the northwest corner would include space for a nursery and washroom facilities. Some of the interior was redesigned as well. Through the front door of the original structure, there was a wide set of central stairs descending to the basement with two side sets of stairs climbing in a winding fashion up to the main auditorium. This was changed to a single side set of stairs descending to the left, a cloakroom to the right and a central set ascending to the main auditorium. This allowed for more seating to be added across the back in a slightly elevated balcony section. A baptistry was built into the front of the church with a set of stairs joining it to the hall of the new addition. The work on the building began in earnest in September. A mortgage was taken out for about $58,000—a large commitment for a small congregation.

---

[24] Trinity Baptist Church, Bulletin, July 1975.

During construction the congregation continued to meet at Trinity Christian School, though their eyes would often turn to the building on Appleby Line with inquiries of how things were progressing. Pioneer Girls, Trinity Boys Club and Intermediate Youth were still very popular on Tuesday evenings and helped the members maintain contact with many families outside the church. As with every local body of believers, there was a need to stay focused on the essential elements of a spiritual Christian walk and practical service for the Lord. At the third anniversary services in October, Pastor Payne reminded the flock that there was more to do than build a better building:

> However, part of our commitment to our church must involve what is sometimes called "outreach." The years ahead of us will demand that all of us seek to reach the lost, to make disciples. We desire to see our church grow and we desire to see it grow by having outsiders become insiders!

With an eye to blending the new with the old, construction and renovation work was completed in six months. So, on Sunday, February 28, 1976, Trinity Baptist Church met for the first time in their new home on Appleby Line, holding an official dedication service that evening. Friends from other sovereign grace churches joined with the congregation to celebrate God's goodness in all He had done to bring this about. This service of praise and dedication drew the congregation together in a special way and they were now set on a road of service to the glory of God in a new neighbourhood and in a new and more permanent home. They rejoiced in the faithful preaching of the Word as brother Leigh Powell, pastor of Covenant Baptist Church, Toronto, delivered an encouraging message of thanksgiving and praise. The church family was now focused on the future and how best to be used in the service of the Lord.

The latter part of the decade

The congregation was now drawing individuals and families from areas outside Burlington, including Milton, Waterdown, Hamilton and Oakville. This growing—but still very young—church family had the advantage of many members who were older in the faith and could steer younger hands in the most fruitful way. That initial zeal in church planting now had to be channelled into the hard work of church maintenance and church growth.

Debt
There was steady progress made in retiring the debt from the church renovations and build. There were two special offerings held each year, one near Easter and the other around the time of the church anniversary in October. These offering times would last for three weeks on each occasion. The board would set a target, usually between $2,500 and $3,500 and, with wonderful regularity, the church family would give and either achieve or exceed the goal. By October 1979 (in just three years), the debt was down from $58,400 to just over $26,000. The Lord's people were giving generously!

Serving
Several new officers were brought onto the board in the late 1970s. Joining Dr. Colin Wellum were elders Don Wheaton, Roy Thompson and George Fager. These men would form the leadership team that would take the church into the next decade. They were gifted by God and used in wonderful ways to encourage the people and offer guidance as the church matured and sought the Lord's leading in terms of outreach and overall ministry. Pennington Ferdinand (Fred) Hambides, Bob Laing, Bob Draper and Joe Schofield were the lead deacons used in the days of growth after moving into the building on Appleby Line. With an older building there was always deaconate work to be done. Joe would be involved in this level of work for decades to come!

Church planting and the training of men for ministry
Members at Trinity were supportive of efforts being made to see solid churches planted, especially in Ontario. In October 1976, a pastoral church planting committee was established with FRPS. The original members were Jim Clemens, Leigh Powell, Roger Fellows and Pastor Payne. By January 1977, they were able to report the following:

> We are pleased that some response has already been made to the letter given out recently concerning support for the Reformed Baptist Church in London where Brian Robinson is the pastor. The desire of the pastors forming the committee heading this effort is that other men should be supported in similar situations to Mr. Robinson and

that, eventually, many new Reformed works should be brought into being. Whether this will ever be achieved depends, under the providence of God, on the support from concerned Christians in various locations.[25]

In April, the church members voted to "endorse in principle the supporting of the establishment of Reformed Baptist Churches in cooperation with the FRPS."[26] Trinity joined the world of "churches supporting churches" very early on and—to God's glory—this has remained a cornerstone of her external financial and prayer support ever since. In the church budget, this became broadly known as Home Missions. Within this new category, the first Church Planting Fund was established in October 1977 to distribute gifts from Trinity. The first church recipient of these funds ($400 per month) was Grace Baptist Church in London, pastored by Brian Robinson. Financial support for this work was also received from other like-minded churches. Pastor Payne offered the following summary statement for the congregation:

> We hope that through this fund other new churches may be established in the future and young men might be encouraged to think in terms of establishing churches in needy areas.

Over the years, there would be many more churches supported in a similar fashion; their pastors and congregations were greatly encouraged by the love and generosity of God's people.[27]

Trinity was always willing to open its doors to the congregations of other works to attend services and meetings held on special occasions. When Trinity arranged for seminars or special speakers, an invitation was sent to all her sister churches with a warm encouragement for them to join. A good example was the fellowship enjoyed at the Good Friday service and fellowship meal where, for many years, people attended from Cottam, Windsor, London and Toronto.

Whenever young men gave evidence of the gifting of God in the world of preaching or teaching, the church felt it was necessary to give these

---

[25] Trinity Baptist Church, Bulletin, Feb. 1977.
[26] Trinity Baptist Church, Business Meeting, April 28, 1976.
[27] See Appendix 4.

men the opportunity to display and develop those gifts. That sentiment is clearly displayed in Pastor Payne's comments to the congregation:

> As God gives us young men who are involved in Bible College or Seminary training, we feel an obligation to give them as much experience in teaching and preaching as their schedule of studies will allow. As a church body we should recognize our obligation in this way and encourage such brethren and make prayerful assessment of their gifts. In line with this, Wilf Ball will preach next Sunday morning. Pray for Wilf that he might know the help of the Spirit of God and that he might be a blessing to all.

Events that nourished and united

The church board and congregation held TBS in high esteem. TBS had a history of faithfulness to the core truths of Scripture and sought, in particular, to train young men for church service and pastoral ministry. There were numerous connections between TBS and Trinity, not the least of which was Pastor Payne having attended there as a student after arriving in Ontario from Liverpool. Each year, the seminary would send out teams of students, usually with Dr. Geoff Adams or one of the professors, to various churches to teach, preach and encourage congregations to remember TBS with prayer and financial support. Invitations were made to attend TBS convocation, graduation and additional events presenting special speakers at Jarvis Street Baptist Church in Toronto. Trinity was always a regular stop on their itinerary.

All regular churchgoers understand there is much more to the life of the congregation than what takes place on Sunday. A variety of opportunities for service, fellowship and outreach arose. The deacons would annually remind the congregation that nothing says spring like a good cleaning-bee at the church. This drew together old and young, gifted and not-so-gifted and, when all was finished, the premises were left clean and in good repair inside and out. Fellowship hours were sometimes held on Saturday afternoons or evenings and often included a film on some relevant topic or individual. One of the favourite genres was that of biographies of key Christians, such as Martin Luther and William Tyndale. Films on instructional topics such as the Dead Sea Scrolls and science/creation were also shown. When the weather was nice in the summer, the congregation would sometimes stay around after the morning service and enjoy a picnic lunch out on the grass around the building. Fellowship hours after evening services would begin at a later date.

One of the most enduring events, however, was the annual Sunday School Picnic, usually held in early June. It was first held in Lowville Park but moved around over the years to local conservation areas like Valen's and Christie's, with later stops at Rehoboth Christian School. Under the leadership of the Sunday School superintendent, there would always be a variety of fun games for all ages, though the adults had to wonder at times if they really wanted to toss that egg or have shaving cream washed off their face with a water pistol at three paces. It was quite horrific to have to view those with beards under those conditions. This was a time when many no-longer-so-youngish people felt their age, as their bodies could not keep pace with the clear, but unreliable, memories of their body from years gone by. This was most painfully displayed in the mass soccer games played with those of stronger and more flexible frame. More than one aging athlete limped off the field shaking their head and promising that would be the last game for them…at least until next year! The fellowship picnic meal usually wrapped up the day with the shared dessert table clearly seen as the highlight. The picnic provided a nice setting for people to sit, relax and enjoy conversation with some they might not usually encounter before or after a regular church service.

The Christmas season provided an opportunity for three very special events. Two gave opportunity to present a clear gospel message of salvation and new life in Christ. Family members and friends who would not normally be in attendance would often attend. First, the Sunday School Christmas Program. Through the bulletin, Pastor Payne encouraged everyone to be part of it:

> This evening the boys and girls of our Sunday School will, in their own special way, bring before us the significance of the Christmas story and the Christmas season. Let us recognize that many of the children, especially the younger ones, have been working on their part of the presentation for some time, and that this is an important activity for them. Encourage them by your presence and pray that the Lord would bless them in the giving, and us in the seeing and hearing, of this special Christmas presentation.

Participation by children was an important aspect of the overall ministry of the church; this was one time when their ministry was front and centre.

Second, there was the Christmas Eve Candlelight Service. Singing and Scripture reading took up most of the time, but the pastor always brought a brief message to focus the hearts and minds of the congregation on the importance of the birth of the Lord Jesus. The lights would be dimmed and candles lit all around the auditorium. The pastor showed himself to be the master of modern technology with his deft handling of his overhead transparencies shining forth on the screen at the front. At times, there was concern for the safety of our pianist as burning candles would occasionally tilt and lean precariously over her head. There were, however, no injuries and the effect of the lighting remains a wonderful memory to many.

Third, at least for a few years, a New Year's Eve Watchnight Service was held. Families would be invited to come late on December 31st to sing, play games, enjoy some refreshments and then welcome in the new year together. There were some young ones who were quietly annoyed because the pastor had a habit of praying as the clock ticked past midnight and they were not able to say, "Happy new year!" until the year was already several minutes old! It was hard, however, to pass up the opportunity to be at the throne of grace as the old and new year connected.

With a concern for the needs of shut-ins and those who missed services for work or illness, an official tape ministry was begun in April 1978. The technical requirements were quite simple, with a portable cassette recorder and mounted microphone fulfilling the task. Faithful men and women served for many years copying, labelling and distributing tapes. One brother eventually collected the cassettes from almost 900 of Pastor Payne's sermons and re-recorded them on CDs. These had to be recorded at normal speed and one at a time. There are now thousands of people worldwide who are indebted to our brother Jacob Kwakernaak and this area of ministry, as those sermons have now been uploaded to Sermon Audio and continue to be downloaded by people being blessed by Pastor Payne's preaching more than twenty-five years after his departure to glory![28]

It is always a good thing for Christians to look back and observe God's hand in what has gone before. Sometimes, in the busyness of church and private life, the role of a loving Father in the day to day is overlooked.

---

[28] https://www.sermonaudio.com/search.asp?SpeakerOnly=true&currSection=sermonsspeaker&keyword=William%5FE%2E%5FPayne.

That is one of the reasons for anniversaries. The official date for Trinity's is the weekend after Thanksgiving, though, due to logistical issues, it is sometimes held a little earlier or later. There have been two main features to the anniversary weekend: the anniversary dinner on Saturday and the ministry of a special speaker for the Saturday evening and both services on Sunday. The banquets, once the church was formally settled on Appleby Line, started out as cramped affairs in the basement hall that had comfortable seating for about thirty or so among the sight-obstructing steel support pillars. There were times when the close fellowship of fifty to sixty upped the temperature a few degrees, but no one complained because it was a celebration of the Lord's goodness for another year. Pastor Payne spoke at the first anniversary weekend but gave up that privilege to a whole host of gifted men over the years.[29] Trinity enjoyed the preaching of men such as John Reisinger, Al Martin, Stuart Olyott, Walter Chantry, Earl Blackburn, Martin Holdt and many others. Thus, the Lord blessed the congregation with exceptional pastoral leadership, as well as with a host of preachers who loved the Word and the Lord of the Word!

Time and space don't allow for all the details relating to youth camping and canoeing trips, weddings, baptisms, chorale evenings and new arrivals that encouraged and some departures that discouraged. Babies were born, saints passed into glory, the Word was preached, and, through God's great mercy, believers grew in grace and the knowledge of the Lord Jesus.

---

[29] See Appendix 6.

3

Early growth and its challenges

The 1980s

◇◇◇◇◇◇◇◇

The church had settled into a solid routine; time and energy were spent improving the programs offered and reaching out in a more significant way to the community nearby. This decade would see consistent growth, another addition, the beginning of new areas of ministry, financial involvement in several works beyond its own and the ongoing development of spiritual maturity.

The burning of the first mortgage

One of the goals of any conservative Baptist church is to become debt free in the shortest time possible, without skimping on the essential areas of church life and ministry along the way. The debt accrued with the first addition and upgrades in 1976 was reduced by generous giving again and again through special offerings. In the five or so years between the loan and its retirement, these generous offerings always exceeded the target. It was this kind of giving that brought the church to its second financial climax (the first being the $30,000 raised to purchase the Zimmerman church outright). During the evening service on March 1, 1981, a rejoicing congregation witnessed the ceremonial burning of the mortgage, "the offending document" as Pastor Payne called it. Dismissing any concern for fire safety, the document was set alight before the entire congregation. Taking part were Robert Laing, treasurer; Dr. Colin Wellum and George Fager, elders; and Fred Hambides, deacon. The final financial push, which had brought in over $6,000, was summarized by the pastor, "This is the remarkable climax—in just six years of endeavour we have achieved, by grace, our goal."

On top of mission support and regular expenses the congregation had contributed over $114,000 toward the building project, broken down as follows:

Cost of original building (paid in full in summer of 1975)	$30,000.00
Payments to contractor for renovations, additions etc in 1975 and 1976	$65,750.00
Bank interest on loan of $58,500	$15,593.22
Balance paid off with this special offering	$ 3,324.16
Total amount raised by the congregation by God's grace	$114,667.38

Anyone who has reached the end of a financial road and can say the debt is now $0 knows how exciting and liberating it can be. The congregation of Trinity could now turn their full financial attention to other matters.

Tenth anniversary (October 1982)

Memorable anniversaries often come in multiples of ten. Much had happened in this first decade. Pastor Payne looked back and highlighted some of the most significant milestones with his usual balance of praise, thankfulness and honour to the Lord:

The Church is yet young and we cannot boast great numbers; but we can say from many points of view, "The LORD has done great things for us whereof we're [sic] glad."[1] One of the most thrilling elements in the brief life of Trinity Baptist Church has been the ways that God has given us an input into the lives of young men whom he has gifted and called to the ministry. Two of our young men are currently pastoring Baptist churches in Ontario; two are involved in theological study with a view to the ministry; and, in this 10th anniversary year we have had the joy of commissioning three of our members for overseas missionary service. For a small church of ten years' existence this has been deeply satisfying and joyous, and there can be no question but that the honour and glory belongs to God alone.

Dr. Al Martin, pastor of Trinity Baptist Church, Essex Falls, New Jersey, was invited to speak and presented a number of messages throughout a special celebratory anniversary week. It was a meaningful time of reflection on the Lord's past goodness and leading, as well as a time to eagerly anticipate His continuing guidance and strength for the challenges and opportunities ahead.

Outreach beyond Trinity

To allow for greater flexibility in connecting with, and supporting, sound ministries outside the church, the Church Planting Fund had been replaced by the Home Missions Fund, allowing application of help to a broader range of ministries. There would be many channels through which support would flow.

The Lord raised up several men with pastoral abilities and gifts in this period. Through the recommendations of Pastor Payne, the church encouraged these men in their pursuit of God's will in their lives as they sought to follow His leading, especially in preaching and church planting. Carl Muller began preaching regularly at Blair Evangelical Baptist Church, a small work just outside Cambridge, Ontario. In late 1981 and early 1982, he and Geof Oprel travelled back and forth to Owen Sound to conduct Bible studies for a couple of families who were interested in establishing a Reformed work in that city. This continued into 1983, at which point

---

[1] Psalm 126:3.

Geof withdrew from that ministry and Carl ministered on his own, while still preaching at Blair. In September 1984, Blair hosted the first annual SGF Picnic and rally for an appreciative crowd from several SGF church families. Not all doors remained open, however, as noted by Pastor Payne in November 1984,

> ...doors are closing and opening...the work in Owen Sound (Geof Oprel then Carl Muller) is closing down. We had to face the fact that the Lord did not appear to be opening such a door at this time in that location, but it appears, in the providence of God, Kirk Wellum is being led into the formation of a new Reformed Baptist work in a developing community between Forest and Sarnia.

In 1985, Carl was called by the congregation at Fundamental Baptist Church in Kingston, Ontario, to be their pastor. He was ordained there on November 23, 1985, with Pastor Payne preaching the ordination message. After his departure from Blair, the work declined to the point that they were preparing to shut down entirely. In early 1986, the remaining members attended a Trinity board meeting and offered to give the church building to Trinity to do with as they saw fit. Some initial discussions about temporarily boarding the place up for safety and then potential sale were put on hold when the possibility of Geof Oprel ministering at Blair was raised. After prayerful consideration, Geof, then an elder at Trinity, offered to step in as interim pastor to see if the work could be revived. By October of that year, Geof took the reins of the church with some start-up funding from the Home Missions Fund of Trinity. The revived work would now be called Grace Bible Church. To help with the transition, Trinity included the financial operations of Grace in their own financial statements until they received their charitable status. Trinity committed a monthly amount to the new work to help supplement the pastor's salary. In April 1987, Grace Bible Church took full possession of their building and began to be reestablished in their community. In June, Geof became the full-time pastor of the work. The Lord had breathed on the embers and a new fire had arisen.

In November 1983, Trinity endorsed the founding of The Sovereign Grace Fellowship of Baptist Churches (SGF), to be formalized at a meeting in London. Clarifying its overall purpose, Pastor Payne noted from the outset,

As was made clear in the proposals this is not a new denomination, but a means of encouraging closer cooperation and fellowship among Baptist Churches committed to either the 1644 or 1689 Baptist Confessions of Faith.

This fellowship is still in full operation at the time of the writing of this history.[2]

In 1985, the church agreed to support Sovereign Grace Community Church (SGCC) in Sarnia on a monthly basis. This was the work overseen by Kirk Wellum after moving from their previous location in Forest. In 1988, they were able to purchase the building that formerly housed Temple Baptist. It was a great encouragement to the folks at Trinity to see the Lord using young men in ministry who had a history with Trinity.

To assist with outreach, as well as those who missed services for sickness, the church purchased a high-speed tape copier. This machine was literally utilized to death, making hundreds of copies of sermons that were distributed far and wide. In May 1987, a copy of *Ultimate Questions* by John Blanchard was first presented to the board and recommended for purchase and distribution. This was to become the most distributed tract by Trinity Baptist Church in the years to come.

With the growing occurrence of abortions in Ontario, it was essential that the church become involved in a meaningful way to oppose it; the offering of alternatives to this awful act was one possibility. In September 1987, a meeting was held to plan for a local crisis pregnancy centre and Pastor Payne was invited to act as chair. This initial meeting culminated in the opening of the Burlington Crisis Pregnancy Centre on November 1, 1989, overseen by Jean Laing as director. God is to be thanked for the way that quiet beginning has been a blessing in saving young lives, first in Burlington and then in Hamilton, as women were finally given options not generally made clear to them in the publicly-funded family counselling arenas. Trinity was one of the first church congregations to get behind these centres and to stay with them through their growing pains and development stages. May the Lord continue to utilize these Christian oases to bless women and their unborn children and to offer counsel to those dealing with post-abortion issues.

---

[2] See https://www.sgfcanada.com.

Some changes of note

Several changes were implemented that would impact the congregation going forward. After having initially used the King James Version (KJV) of the Bible for worship and study at Trinity until 1983, the board, with a strong lead from Pastor Payne, recommended the use of the New King James Version (NKJV) in all areas of worship (becoming the pew Bible in early 1985). The updated language was considered beneficial to general understanding and study by the congregation at large. It was deemed an excellent translation, true to the original texts and still vibrant in its makeup.

In that same year, in an outreach effort to the local community, some members distributed the first issue of *Trinity Tidings*. This was a general evangelical paper with a section dedicated to our local church, introducing us and encouraging people in the community to come out. A couple hundred copies were taken door to door, four times a year for several years. There were one or two individuals who came to the church through this process, but the overall response was minimal and the ministry eventually ceased. Pastor Payne, always ready to offer reality checks when needed, noted in a bulletin in June 1988,

> This is not a glamourous work and does not produce spectacular results, but God will use it in His own way. Keep up the good work.

A ministry specifically directed at the needs of men was introduced in December—a men's breakfast. This became a regular source of meaningful teaching and fellowship with many outside speakers addressing the men on a wide range of "manly" topics over the years. The food was always enjoyable, though the building of relationships through discussion and regular conversation was an even greater blessing.

In 1984, to help the hearing impaired, the church, installed the Phonic Ear System. Several members made successful use of it; there was now no reason not to be fully engaged with the services! To encourage people to attend mid-week prayer meetings in the winter months, regional prayer locations were established in Milton, Burlington and Waterdown. The hospitality shown by so many church families helped make these meetings times of close fellowship and intimate corporate prayer. In June 1985, the evening service was moved ahead by 30 minutes to 6:30 p.m.—a radical alteration in schedule that did not produce any world-altering cataclysm!

Faithful prayer warriors

It is wonderful to see a group of believers rally around a theme for prayer, and a faithful and dedicated group of women in Milton did just that. On Tuesday mornings, they gathered to pray, initially and primarily for unbelieving family members, but also for the church and its people and ministries. Many of them had come to faith later in life and were burdened for the souls of their older children who were not walking with the Lord. Most had been members of Emmanuel Baptist Church in Milton but left when the church battled its way through issues that caused a split in the membership and some families ended up at Trinity. It was at this juncture that many of their children walked away from the church.

In addition to their prayerfulness, they would sign and send cards to people who were sick, with heart-warming encouragements and passages of Scripture to cheer their hearts. Perhaps in glory, the extent of their intercession on behalf of so many will be made known. The main body of this group, lovingly referred to as the "Milton Ladies," included Ina Bissel, Freda DeBoer, Hilda Skinner, Jeanne Walden, Peg Draper, Molly Charlton, Eloise Meikle, June Thomson and Rita Van de Merwe. They even welcomed a couple of the younger moms, Jackie Ball and Merry-Lynn Hudson, to join them. As part of the social aspect of their meetings, however, they did insist on one particularly important, unalterable rule: when it came to drinking tea at refreshment time, it could only be served in china cups. Long live civilized behaviour!

The mission field

On April 1, 1984, the church bid farewell to the Ball family as they headed to Zaire as missionaries. Wilf, Jackie and the girls made up the first family sent out to the mission field as members of Trinity. It was one of those paradoxical joyful and sad times—they were off to do what the Lord had prepared them to do, but they would be greatly missed by the entire congregation. Missions were always a top priority when it came time to determine how church resources would be utilized. With the October budget, the church was offering about $1,200 per month in total support for the Tiessens, Greens, Gordons, Surpless's, Balls and Pikkerts. This represented about 25 per cent of the total church budget. This pattern of giving generously to work beyond Trinity's own geographical location remained a top priority through the years.[3] In celebration of the work of missions, Trinity held its first Missions Weekend on March 23–24, 1985, featuring Dr. Terry Tiessen as the special speaker. At this conference, among several key exhortations, the reminder to pray as well as to give was a point of great emphasis.

Another extension

Numerical growth in a congregation is usually a good thing, especially if the Lord is seen to be at work in that growth. In a fixed space, it also has its challenges, and that involves being creative in developing additional space. At the November 1985 board meeting, the first discussions were had regarding another extension to the existing building. The nursery was too small for all the children in it and a more contained room (other than the main auditorium) for fellowship and prayer meetings would be very welcome. In early 1986, things moved ahead rapidly with plans for the construction of an office, new washrooms, a prayer room/fellowship hall and nursery extension. By May, final costs had been estimated at between $60,000 and $65,000. A proposal was made to the church members and, with 25 voting Yes, 5 voting No and 4 abstentions, the plan was approved. The Lord graciously intervened and, in reasonably short order, permits were granted and the site plan approved. Of course, being a designated historical building produced additional complications with respect to obtaining permits. The church would have to stay within the appearance restrictions laid down by the city committees. They wanted to ensure the addition "looked" like it belonged to the overall structure. The board felt it could operate within the parameters laid out for them and proceeded with planning. In addition, variance had to be obtained to allow additional building on a lot size that was too small for a church; permission was requested and granted from the Niagara Escarpment Commission (NEC) to build as near as 35 feet from the top of the Bronte Creek ravine. A dry hydrant was installed on the water cistern to allow firefighters access to a water supply in case of fire. A building committee was established, and work got underway in October. In November, the church agreed to borrow $60,000 from the Bank of Montreal—a mortgage was once again on the books. With the help of men within the congregation, the extension,

---

[3] See Appendix 3.

referred to as the "wing," was soon completed. It was dedicated at the evening service on February 22, 1986. By August, $5,000 had been paid on the loan and, through special offerings twice a year, was reduced to $30,000 by June 1988, and completely retired by September 1989! The Lord, being always good, developed in His people a spirit of generosity and sacrifice when it came to His work. Trinity had been blessed with great givers since its inception.

What about additional land?

Early in 1988, Pastor Payne introduced to the board the idea of purchasing additional land on the north side of No. 2 Sideroad (No. 2 SR) as a starting point for possible future expansion. At first, the board was hesitant and took some convincing to seriously consider this idea. However, upon examining the plans for the new 407 highway that would run just south of the church (to be completed in the far distant year of 2000), the board became intrigued. In October 1988, land prices off No. 2 SR were estimated at about $150,000 for three acres. That seemed quite high, but then, in November, the board was informed the owner would be willing to sell at $20,000 per acre for up to four acres, which represented the "farm price" for the land. This seemed much more reasonable based on the church budget, though there were still long discussions related to taking on any additional debt while the previous extension had still not been paid off. To include the congregation in the process, a letter was sent out in December where the pastor proposed the following for their prayerful consideration:

> First, I want to share with you the thoughts of your elders and deacons over the past few months. We have felt the need to look ahead as a church. It is important to have a vision for the future. We all know that our church building is very rurally located, and it is likely that the authorities will try to keep this area a "green belt" area. However, we should be aware of the fact that important developments are being planned not too far to the south of us in the future. The extension of the 403 highway [now 407] is planned for just South of No. 1 SR. It is likely that an interchange will be built at Appleby Line. This will provide fast and easy access to our church from east and west. Furthermore, Burlington homes are continuing to move north and eventually there will be some housing developments around Appleby

and No. 5 Highway. This will be a challenge for evangelism and hopefully holds the prospect of new families being attracted to the church.

On some Sundays there have been few seats available. But we have to think ahead, even to the coming generation. Should we not have faith to believe that in the years ahead we shall need a larger building? Ought we not to begin to plan for this now?'

The board's decision on whether to proceed was also being influenced by an offer from persons within the church to cover the entire cost of the land purchase of four acres. If the land could be purchased, then the next item would be to decide what and where to build. Would a new auditorium be built to hold 250 or 350? Would it be built as part of the present structure or would the church look to move and build an entirely new structure on the newly acquired land? These were great questions. However, any further discussion was put on hold when additional inquiries with the owner of the land began to be ignored and go unanswered. In the meantime, additional space for seating would have to found by juggling the present spaces as cleverly as possible. Looking ahead in faith, though, the board began exploring the possibility of building a major extension on the present site. With these details presented to the members at a business meeting in February 1989, the church agreed to pursue the purchase of four acres across No. 2 SR for $20,000 per acre. The wait for a reply from the owner would take some time.

Exhortations of encouragement by Pastor Payne

Pastor Payne would often include notes of encouragement in the bulletin that dealt with various aspects of church life and ministry. A few have been included here to give the reader a flavour of what was on his heart and in his mind as pastor of the flock at Trinity. He did not want to overlook those essential elements at the core of the work, which could easily be taken for granted.

1. Prayer

> If we are not a praying church we shall not be a blessed church. Never forget that the enemy of your soul and the enemy of this testimony will always aim at making us a prayerless people. We must understand

this and realize that in order to thwart him we must discipline ourselves and commit ourselves to gathering for prayer just as often as we possibly can.[4]

2. Workers in the church

It is surely fitting from time to time to recognize the fine work being done by our Sunday School teachers and our youth leaders, as week after week they prepare their lessons and faithfully present the Word of God to young minds. This is an unglamorous, plodding kind of work which can often be discouraging. But it is a work of great importance which the Lord will undoubtedly honour. Those engaged in it should be remembered in prayer by the rest of the congregation and helped and supported in every way possible. We express our appreciation to our faithful workers; let us all work with them by praying for the blessing of God upon the seed of truth sown in young minds. This too is a vital aspect of the work which must not be overlooked.[5]

3. Worship

Once again we have the privilege of gathering to worship God and to hear His Word together. Let us remember again how important it is to give ourselves to concentrated, intelligent and wholehearted worship. To worship God in a sleepy, halfhearted manner is insulting to God and unworthy of Him. Let each of us contribute our part to worship which is alive and vibrant and a blessing to us all.[6]

4. Mothers

We honour all mothers today, but especially those Christian mothers who seek to prepare their children not only for time but for eternity. May such mothers always have strength to resist the pressures of the world and be obedient to the Word of God.[7]

---

[4] Trinity Baptist Church, Bulletin, Dec. 1984.
[5] Trinity Baptist Church, Bulletin, Feb. 1985.
[6] Trinity Baptist Church, Bulletin, March 1985.
[7] Trinity Baptist Church, Bulletin, May 1985.

5. Fellowship
Church fellowship groups had just been introduced.

> It is really important that each of us should see the importance of fellowship among the members of the congregation. It is a most positive and wholesome thing for us to relax with one another and get to know one another, to share each other's joys and burdens. The fellowship groups have been drawn up to assist in this process and we hope that those involved in them will get to work with them.[8]

6. Social ills

> Now is the time to let our elected representatives know that we care about the slaughter of unborn children. Take a few minutes and write your MP.[9]

7. Vision

> Sometimes Christians have a cramped and restricted outlook when it comes to the cause of Christ. They know about their own church and perhaps have some understanding of what is happening in their own country, but that is it; nothing more. All Christians ought to be vitally interested in what God is doing all over the world; we ought to be concerned about the spread of Christ's kingdom everywhere. Therefore, when literature is available giving details of the Lord's work in other places, we should make use of it.[10]

8. Humour
And, not to lose sight of his sense of humour:

> Please note that the Ladies Meeting will be held on May 9th, not May 2nd, as previously planned. Premier Miller is to blame of course, having called an election for May 2nd without consulting our ladies. We shall forgive the premier for this blunder, but we trust that the

---

[8] Trinity Baptist Church, Bulletin, Nov. 1989.
[9] MP means Member of Parliament. Trinity Baptist Church, Bulletin, Sept. 1989.
[10] Trinity Baptist Church, Bulletin, March 1989.

Ladies will be sure to note the change in date.[11]

As the church approached its fifteenth anniversary, the pastor distributed a letter to the congregation. His comments covered the usual balanced spectrum. In part, it read:

> As I consider our 15th anniversary as a church, I am personally deeply moved. How good is the God we adore! How faithful He has been down the years, and what blessings He has bestowed upon us. We have seen men and women and young people come to faith in Christ; we have seen them confess their faith in the beautiful ordinance of baptism; we have seen God's people instructed and helped, strengthened and matured in the Christian life; we have seen young people go forth to serve the Lord Jesus in various parts of the world. We have a fellowship that is, I believe, united and loving and strong. For all of this we can only say, "All glory be to God"; for "Unless the LORD guards the city, the watchman stays awake in vain."[12]
>
> Of course, to use the old biblical phrase, "There remains yet much land to be possessed."[13] We have a long way to go, and the spiritual and discerning eye will see many areas of weakness and concern. We are yet a young church, and we are still a small church; we must have vision and faith for the future. Mercy drops have fallen around us, and we bless God for that, as it is all of His grace, but we must yet plead for the showers....Is it not necessary for us to be continually renewing our commitment—first to our beloved Lord, and then to this testimony we call Trinity Baptist Church? Devotion can die; zeal can cool; support can waver; love can cease. In terms of our spirituality and our commitment to Christ's cause, it behooves us all to "be sober and vigilant,"[14] to "watch and pray."[15]

One final note regarding the broadening work of Pastor Payne. Having already enjoyed a long connection to Toronto Baptist Seminary, he was invited to join their teaching staff in the fall of 1989, where he taught

---

[11] Trinity Baptist Church, Bulletin, May 1985.
[12] Psalm 127:1 NKJV.
[13] See Joshua 13:1.
[14] 1 Peter 5:8.
[15] Matthew 26:41. Trinity Baptist Church, pastoral letter, Fall 1989.

courses in pastoral theology and homiletics. His experience, wisdom, knowledge and example would be used to help shape the ministries of many young men who had the privilege to sit under his tutelage. His teaching, preaching and counsel was a blessing to Trinity as well as to individuals and groups much further afield. This breadth of influence went hand-in-hand with his preaching and teaching ministry at conferences and special meetings in Canada, the USA and Europe.

The second decade closed with the congregation and leadership displaying a strong sense of hopefulness and excitement at the prospects before them. The 1990s would be a time of great rejoicing, as well as deep sadness, where the richness and abundance of God's grace would be needed in a particularly special and personal way.

4

Coming of age

The 1990s

◇◇◇◇◇◇◇◇

Overview

Since it is only possible to highlight a few events in the space allowed, the spotlight cannot fall on all the good works performed by and through the people of Trinity, works prepared long beforehand by the Lord to be done to His glory.[1] The people continued to be equipped through the sound preaching and teaching of the Word of God, unbelievers were challenged to turn from their sin to new life in Jesus Christ and a thousand individual deeds were performed that only the Lord knows. Investment was made in other works, either well established or new and emerging; sometimes financially, often in prayer and occasionally with the offer of free labour. The small work at

---

[1] See Ephesians 2:10.

Blair received extensive attention for many years and eventually blossomed forth as Grace Bible Church in Cambridge, still a thriving body of believers. Ministries such as the Burlington Crisis Pregnancy Centre, new overseas mission endeavours, video-taping of messages for shut-ins and monthly public broadcast, Maple Villa Seniors Home visitation, student teams from TBS, full day instructional seminars, a new ladies Bible study group, the ever prayerful Milton Ladies and many others were all integral pieces of the work of the church as a whole. Though not discussed in detail, these were key threads woven into the overall fabric of what Trinity was at her core—a proclaimer of the whole gospel, by word and deed, in formal and informal settings. Sometimes even a specific, though unexpected, event would hasten the development of a needed strategy or protocol. For example, the exciting electrical fire in the baptistry revealed the immediate need of a much-improved fire evacuation plan; one in which people actually leave the building when there is fire and smoke!

Dealing for land

A summary letter, dated March 23, 1991, was sent out by the board to the members; it brought into sharp focus the results of almost two years of discussion, debate, prayer and exploration. One of the key pieces of information to emerge was that the land for sale by Mrs. Krysek was no longer going at "farm price" ($20,000 per acre—where the church had hoped to purchase up to 4 acres); the land would be going for a more residential/business price. Thus, 1.5 acres was now going to cost about $165,000! This shift in price resulted in renewed discussion as to the best route forward for the church.

A special business meeting was held for members on Wednesday, April 10, 1991, where the idea of purchasing that additional land over No. 2 SR was discussed. The desire of the board was that all possible avenues of moving forward would be open to dialogue and feedback. The pastor urged the members to deal with differences of opinion on the matter with respect and grace, as initial general feedback indicated unanimity did not seem likely. From the pastor, "Let's commit ourselves to accepting graciously whatever decision is forthcoming, even if it is not our personal preference. I pledge myself to this." To confirm a spirit of unity on the matter, a level of 75 per cent support was established as the threshold for acceptance.

The various options for proceeding were laid out by the board:

1. *Do nothing at all*. This did not seem to be a responsible or wise way of proceeding.
2. *Start a new work*. In principle this commends itself to us and our hope is that it will become a reality in the future. The pastor's philosophy is not in favour of the megachurch approach. However, there are some things to consider:
    a. There is truth to the old saying that there is strength in numbers. Together we have been able to do many good things which we may not have been able to do without numerical strength.
    b. One good sized work is better than two or three struggling, small works. Starting a new work these days is a tough and often discouraging task.
    c. A new work would only postpone the issue because ultimately a new work would require its own land and building.
    d. A new work elsewhere would not solve the problems of providing for the future needs of the present work.
3. *Purchase another building*. This is great where it can be done, but appropriate buildings are very hard to come by in the Burlington area.
4. *Make changes to our present building*. This is an attractive suggestion, but given our present situation there are problems. Even if we could enlarge it to make it worthwhile, we would still need extra land for parking. Other problems: how much "knocking about" the present building could stand; in enlarging the present auditorium we would anticipate an eventual substantial increase in the congregation and yet not have enlarged parallel facilities for ministries such as nursery and Sunday school.
5. *Find a new location altogether*. The problem here is that we would then be into even more expense. It would not be wise to move further North, and the cost of land to the South is extremely high.

There were additional reasons expressed in favour of the land purchase at this point:

- purchase of land at this time would not commit the church to an early building project
- leading up to a potential build might require two services in the morning temporarily

- there is a window of opportunity to purchase now that may not exist in the future
- with the pledge of a very generous gift, the land purchase would not have a major impact on the budget (the giver was anonymous, but the gift offered was $100,000)

With this information in hand, the congregation was given two weeks to prayerfully consider the options. The follow-up meeting was held on April 24, 1991, for the people's decision.

At the meeting the pastor took the time to recap the reasons for considering land purchase at the present time, referring to the congregational letter of March 23rd and the discussions from April 10th. A presentation was made by deacon Joe Schofield in which he outlined the contacts made with Mrs. Krysek, as well as with Mr. Cooke who owned the land on the east side of Appleby Line across from the church building (another, less desirable piece of property). Joe had also met with various town officials, including the NEC, to sound them out on possible building expansion on the present property and land use on the north lot. He showed the members plans that included a large potential addition to the north side of the present facility, onto the green space beside the church building, presently used for the septic bed. Emphasis was placed on efforts to keep costs low, but any building project would involve a significant price tag.

In the follow-up discussion three valid concerns emerged:

1. Would it be best to build on the present site or purchase land elsewhere and build an entirely new facility?
2. Would the church be pressured by the town into a commitment never to sell the land on No. 2 SR should it be purchased?
3. Will the church be granted permission to build an addition on the present site?

Regarding the first, a number of men in the church directly involved in the building trade recommended going after a minimum of 2 acres, but eventually pursuing an addition on the present site. This was largely based on the church's present financial situation and the price of land elsewhere. For the second item, the board was firm in its commitment not to agree to never selling. In addition, relating to the third concern, the purchase of land would be conditional on receiving assurance from the city that

Trinity would be able to build on its present site. There were many other thoughtful questions asked and answered regarding details related to septic beds, parking, set-backs, severance, permits, etc. However, with the city planning department showing little support for the project at this point, it seemed the severance of the land and related permits to build would only materialize if the Lord was indeed in it!

The members gathered again on May 1st and voted in favour of a proposal where the church would offer $70,000 per acre for two acres but be willing to go as high as $165,000 in total. Pastor Payne summarized the situation in the bulletin of May 5:

> The proposal to put in an offer to purchase land at the corner of Appleby Line and #2 Side Road was accepted by the church with an 88% majority at the business meeting last Wednesday. This of course does not guarantee our getting the land. The "powers that be" in the city of Burlington have expressed themselves very negatively concerning our getting severance of the land. However, our desire is that God's will be done and thus we commit the matter to Him in the confidence that, "He does all things well!" Pray that the Lord will have His way and make it clear to us as we follow the process through.[2]

There would be a hiatus in the proceedings as the church awaited a response from the seller; a concrete offer was ready when and if they opened the door to sell.

In early 1992, the deacons were once again in contact with Mrs. Krysek, discussing the possible purchase of the land. An official offer sheet was sent to her in late January with an offer of $140,000 for 2 acres, extending 280 feet along Appleby Line and 310 feet on No. 2 SR. There were several conditions attached to the offer, including a list of additional expenses related to land transfer and who should be responsible for paying them. A month later she presented a counteroffer asking for $155,000 for 2 acres, extending 436.5 feet on Appleby Line and 200 feet on No. 2 SR. Most of the extra costs were tossed back to Trinity with the additional stipulation that land use would be limited to parking only. This would preclude ever building on this parcel of land. On April 6th, however, a counteroffer was made to Mrs. Krysek for $147,500, with Trinity covering the costs

---

[2] Trinity Baptist Church, Bulletin, May 5, 1991.

for severance, variance and separation, while she would cover the survey cost; there would be no land use stipulation. The offer, with some slight modifications, was finally accepted and the sale moved forward. Trinity would soon have its plot of land. At the very least, it would be used for additional parking, as the city now seemed more favourable to allowing an addition to be built onto the existing church structure. The original desire of Pastor Payne had simply been to give a future generation the option of growth if the Lord so allowed. The foundation for expansion was now laid, but it would be another twelve years before an addition opened for its first service.

The generous benefactor gave the church the gift of $100,000 for the purchase of the land in two parts; $30,000 was sent as a cheque to the church and $70,000 was set aside in a trust account to be used when the land sale was completed. Understandably, if the sale did not go through all monies would be returned to the donor.

The Lord allowed the church to overcome numerous obstacles that could have abruptly stopped the sale: there was the announcement of a moratorium on development in North Burlington in early 1993 that would prevent a new addition; the NEC noted the farmland under consideration had already reached its limit for severances; building at this time ran contrary to the regional plan for the area; there was insufficient water for firefighting; an addition would be too close to the ravine; plus various challenges related to set-backs, building size and zoning by-laws. One by one, these issues were brought before city council and its various committees. In God's time, and by His mercy, all the obstacles and contrary arguments were overcome. An exemption from the building moratorium required a written application to the city, followed by an oral presentation to the city council. Deacons Joe Schofield and Fred Hambides represented the church before the council and a public gallery full of people. Joe did the speaking and Fred did the praying; the Lord graciously gave courage to Joe and an answered prayer to Fred as an exemption to the building moratorium was granted.

In addition, the Lord allowed the following situations to be cleared up: the new property was re-zoned to allow for a septic field bed; firefighting water storage could be provided through underground storage tanks on the new property; parking would be permitted; strips of land along the two major roadways were ceded to the city as road allowance; a maximum footprint for the potential addition was agreed upon; all the necessary variances were obtained. After settling the distance limits of a new footprint for an extension, a conditional site plan covering both lots was submitted and approved. Finally, permits were obtained to install a septic line under No. 2 SR and to allow the driveway and north sidewalk entry onto No. 2 SR. It seemed clear that the Lord was directing the church toward her goal.

Now the purchase of the land needed to be finalized; that process had its own wrinkles and took some additional time to accomplish. At least it was known that expansion of the building could take place when the time was right.

Leaving aside many of the final details, it is enough to say that negotiations between seller and buyer involved some additional give and take on both sides. It was not until November 1994 that the land deal officially closed—the property finally belonged to Trinity. The church had all but $15,000 of the selling price of $147,500 on hand. A loan of $55,000 was taken on by the church: $15,000 for the sale amount and $40,000 to develop the land for parking (a loan that would be repaid by November 1997). This would include curbs, lights, hydro, the line for a future septic system, sidewalks and so on. The city also required a $55,000 line of credit to be used by them if the appropriate site plan work was not completed. In other words, if the sidewalks and curbing were not done voluntarily, it would be done at the church's expense by the city. Apparently, the city was not used to working with the likes of the deacons at Trinity.

Work was to begin almost immediately, with the hope that the lot could be functioning through the winter months. However, winter itself slowed progress, along with the usual planning and execution delays. It wasn't until October 1995 that the culverts were installed and work on the surface of the lot was underway. A suggestion that about twenty trees be planted in the lot space was declined, but the surface of the lot was prepared for use. The immediate priority was adequate lighting which was met with the installation of several lighting poles spread throughout the lot. Sidewalks and curbs would not be in until June 1997. The north lot was now functioning as it had been envisioned. The extra space alleviated a lot of stress on the south parking area which would now be reserved for the elderly and families with young children.

The board had recommended to the church family that once the land had been purchased (priority 1) then plans for building an addition to the present church building could be explored more fully, with the express purpose of getting a building up in a timeframe that fit the church budget. For this to happen, everyone looked to the Lord with faith and anticipation. The site plan approval was good for five years. It would have to be extended, however, to allow the new addition to finally be built.

Overcrowding and its challenges

As has been noted, it became apparent that space in the main auditorium would one day be insufficient for the size of the congregation. Discussions within the board examined possible short-term solutions such as the addition of a row of chairs, the construction of a balcony at the back, running two morning services, setting up overflow seating in the basement and restructuring the room to allow for more seats. It was at this time that the suggestion of adding an entirely new auditorium to the facility was first introduced and discussed. The initial plan included seating for up to 400 (with a balcony); an initial cost was pegged at about $650,000. At the end of some lengthy discussions, this idea seemed beyond the present means and needs and was temporarily shelved, though the plan never went away and would, in the Lord's long-term direction for Trinity, eventually become a reality.

Some solutions were implemented beginning with a restructuring of the front of the auditorium. In February 1993, parts of the large platform at the front were removed and replaced with seating, allowing for an additional twenty-one people. Set at 90° to the pulpit, the new seating had the appearance of an Anglican church choir loft, but the extra space was greatly appreciated. Chairs were sometimes added at the back and in the main aisle, but removal was always a bit tricky at the end of the service and it is doubtful the fire marshall would have approved. Once this new space began to fill, however, it seemed prudent to invite professional contractors in to give their assessment on a possible new auditorium.

A single camera was installed at the back of the auditorium to capture video recordings for shut-ins. As an added benefit, the video feed allowed for an overflow space downstairs when the main auditorium reached capacity. Soon, Trinity became a multi-camera facility which allowed for different camera angles of the preacher and congregation. A TV was brought in, chairs set up and individuals and families began to voluntarily go downstairs when the upstairs filled up or appeared to be filling up; the timing of this was not always smooth. The singing was a challenge, as the organ and piano in real life gave a much better lead than even full volume on the TV set would allow. It is a strange phenomenon that, when people begin to hear their own voice singing, their tendency is to sing quieter when singing louder would be more conducive to congregational worship in that downstairs space. However, in spite of the hurdles, the overflow room became a regular part of the morning service. To avoid having the same people down there all the time (all the young people for instance!), rotating rosters of volunteers took their turn so space upstairs would always be available to visitors. Toward the end of the decade there were, on average, about twenty-five people downstairs for the service. Having a split congregation is never a healthy situation in the long-term. Discussions on church planting, building or moving ratcheted up once again. The church did not imagine, however, the plans the Lord had in mind waiting just around the corner.

On February 1, 1999, Don Theobald left Binbrook Baptist Church, after eighteen years of service there, to become the pastor of the newly formed Pilgrim Baptist Fellowship in Ancaster. He began his formal pastoral work among the brothers and sisters there two weeks later. Over the next few months, several individuals and families left Trinity to become part of this new work. Official church farewells were made to those who were going, along with the prayer that they would be used wonderfully within that work. At first it was two individuals and three families (some who lived in the Ancaster area), but, eventually, almost forty in total made the move. This was a difficult time for the congregation and the leadership at Trinity, as friendships built up over the years made these partings painful on many levels. However, workers were needed at Pilgrim and, as a result, the need for overflow space at Trinity was lifted for a time; in some ways a win for both congregations. The new workers were a tremendous blessing to the fledgling work and the Lord soon had that church growing and thriving.

Trinity Times

There are so many different storylines arising within a church at any given time it is a challenge to stay on top of them so they might be adequately prayed for and properly appreciated. To help keep the church informed on issues that would not be covered in the weekly bulletin, several enterprising writers and designers asked for permission to create a church paper entitled *Trinity Times*. The goal was to go to press quarterly, though this timetable was not always achievable. The *Trinity Times* began around

1990 and had a good run until the mid-90s when it went into temporary hibernation. It was picked up again in early 1997, with a new editorial staff and ran at least until the end of the decade. During its printing history, more than twenty editions were published and distributed to members of the congregation. They were well thought out, targetted a wide range of readers and quickly became a much-anticipated source of information, instruction and even entertainment.

A variety of topics were covered through articles on the family, special celebrations such as Christmas and Easter, historical events and figures, biblical doctrines, information items related to the church and the SGF, mission news, travelogues, poetry, promotions for upcoming events, hymnology, items for prayer and complete messages from the pastor and other preachers. Testimonials were a regular feature as members were able to express their thanksgiving for God's mercy and goodness, especially in times of trial and challenge. These insights into the souls of the people provided an opportunity to get to know others in a deeper and more understanding way and to remind one another that a believer's life is filled with challenges, with a mix of failures and victories, here and around the world. Recipes were always a highlight and formed the foundation for many fine meals, with special desserts receiving particular praise! Word games and puzzles appeared regularly for children and children-at-heart. Contributions arose from a cross section of the congregation and included men, women, boys and girls. Articles and artwork represented the many gifts afforded the people by the Holy Spirit, as they were given a channel through which to express their ideas and observations. Modified versions were sometimes produced and distributed to the local neighbourhood as an evangelistic tool. The *Trinity Times* did much to lift the spirits of all its readers and help bind them together in fellowship.

One of the most looked-for highlights was a cleverly drawn cartoon entitled, "Liverpool Lexicon" and starred Pastor Payne. The artist was a little shy, especially as the content often painted the pastor in a humorous way; the identity of the artist was never publicly revealed—until now—don't tell anyone, but it was Wilf Ball, an elder at the church at the time! The cartoon drawing usually represented one of Pastor Payne's verbal idiosyncrasies, as his Liverpudlian vocabulary often seemed "interestingly odd" to those without a similar accent or cultural background.

These issues took a tremendous amount of time to piece together and produce. Many of the sermons that appeared were painstakingly typed out from cassette recordings by those who typed much slower than the pastor preached. The rewind button was the first part of the device to wear out! The dedication of the editors is to be commended; this was a work that blessed all its readers many times over.

Communicating with the people

When a note of concern needed to be sounded, the pastor would use any means at his disposal to get out his message. At a time when congregational prayer seemed at a low ebb, he addressed the people through the bulletin,

> Let us remember that we are engaged in a real spiritual warfare not only in our own land of Canada but reaching to the ends of the earth. Are we concerned to see revival in our day? Are we concerned to see the Lord move in the conversion of sinners and the strengthening of His people? Are we concerned to see our missionaries encouraged and made fruitful? Then we must come together as a people committed to united, fervent intercession. Let's give ourselves to prayer and trust the Lord for blessing.[3]

He wrote many letters to his congregation back at Calvary, as well as some in the 1980s to Trinity. It was in October 1991, however, that he undertook this task again, with the intent of issuing them at least quarterly, though there were interruptions in their sequence and regularity due to a variety of issues and circumstances that arose, not the least of which pertained to the pastor's health. In these letters, Pastor Payne would communicate ideas, share plans from the board for the church family and exhort them to stay the course in Christian service. He also introduced new ministries for consideration by the congregation, such as the International Fellowship of Reformed Baptists (IFRB). He addressed the act of giving as a means of worship when costs were up and offerings were down; he extolled the virtue and blessing of active hospitality among the people and even made recommendations on how to make the most out of a summer vacation. He encouraged attention to, and participation in, special events such as church anniversaries, as well as regular and energetic adherence to the weekly services of the church. Sometimes the

---

[3] Trinity Baptist Church, Bulletin, Apr. 1993.

letter was largely informational, such as sharing updates on the ongoing work on the potential purchase of land. Others focused on the great need to pursue our commitment to missions without losing heart.

In his November 1992 letter, he exhorted the people to greater faith in God, when he stated,

> Let us consider the importance of faith. Many an individual life is spiritually barren simply through lack of faith in God and His promises. Many a church is deprived of blessing for the same reason. God loves to see His people exercising faith in Him; faith honours God and He delights in it. Faith sees God's promises as trustworthy; and when a church has confidence in God a spirit of hope and expectation is born. Faith gives rise to praise and inspires prayer; God always honours it. God grant the spirit of faith to our congregation.[4]

The letters were put on hold in the mid-90s, but, providentially, they were revived in 1997. Their purpose is given in his first letter in 1997:

> I hope that it might be possible to issue this kind of brief pastoral letter several times each year, and thus revive a practice which we used to engage in some years ago. In this way items of news can be passed along, matters relating to the life of our congregation and the wider work of the kingdom can be shared, and items of encouragement or concern may be provided. Hopefully, the pastoral letter may prove to be one means among others to contribute toward a sense of unity and togetherness within our congregation.[5]

In the first half of that year, only two letters were written, the final one coming in the spring. In what was to be his final communication in this form to the congregation, he focused on Zechariah 4:6, "'Not by might nor by power, but by My Spirit,' says the LORD of hosts" (NKJV). He stated,

> They remind us that in seeking to build the kingdom of God His people must always and only rely upon the Spirit of God....It is He who is the true teacher of the things of Christ; it is He who sanctifies

---

[4] Trinity Baptist Church, pastoral letter, Nov. 1992.
[5] Trinity Baptist Church, pastoral letter, Winter 1997.

God's people and who convicts of sin, righteousness and judgement. He is the Spirit of grace and supplication and He Who gives power to those who are weak in and of themselves. Let us not grieve Him by disunity, prayerlessness, lack of love toward the Lord Jesus, spiritual carelessness or any other sin, but rather wholeheartedly devote ourselves to honouring Him so that His presence may increasingly be known among us. Oh, that in this 25th anniversary year we might know a greater and ever-increasing measure of the Spirit's grace, blessing and power. Unitedly, let us pray earnestly to that end.
In His grace, W.E. Payne.[6]

God prepares for the future

When Carl and Heather Muller and their family returned to the Ancaster area after four years pastoring in Kingston, it seemed an excellent idea to utilize his spiritual training, experience and capable leadership within his new home church. In May 1990, the elders held their first discussions on bringing Carl on as an assistant to Pastor Payne, who, at that time, was being offered more and more opportunities to minister to other pastors and church leaders through conferences and preaching engagements. The elders recognized Pastor Payne's unique gifts that allowed him to offer balanced and practical leadership, instruction, encouragement and counsel to men and congregations far beyond the walls of Trinity. Being instrumentally used at the heart of the Reformed movement in Canada at its earliest stages, had granted Pastor Payne a connection to dozens of like-minded men in North America and around the world. He needed to be freed up to be used in a broader field of service. Inviting Carl to help with preaching and visitation, Pastor Payne would be able to commit more time and energy to this very essential extended ministry. It was not difficult to convince the membership. In October 1990, Carl was voted in as an elder and as assistant pastor, a position in which he served faithfully for the next seven years. No one knew at that point that the Lord would use this time to prepare Carl for a more daunting and challenging level of service at Trinity.

---

[6] Trinity Baptist Church, pastoral letter, Spring 1997.

Signs of wear and tear

As often happens, when nothing special seems to be happening, the unexpected happens. Because of his own history, and that of family members, it was not a complete surprise when, in late May 1994, Pastor Payne experienced a sudden onset of fatigue and a feeling of being very unwell while he was in the pulpit preaching. He requested Pastor Muller to step in, as he did not have the strength to finish his sermon. He went home to rest; the following day, in line with God's amazing mercy and care, he suffered his second heart attack while in the doctor's office. After further, extensive examination it was determined he needed surgery to repair the damage to his heart. While he awaited surgery, Carl stepped in to take on a good portion of the preaching load, though men from other churches were also called on to help shoulder that burden. Pastor Payne rested from work for the next couple of months. He returned to a somewhat reduced load of preaching, teaching and chairing church meetings in September.

To show that the board had not lost its sense of humour during his absence, in a discussion on the necessity of considering safety first, it was noted in the September meeting minutes,

> The TV is going to be put up in the lower auditorium in the near future. We are guaranteed it will not fall on anyone important.

In the minutes of the annual general business meeting (AGBM) in October, Pastor Payne noted the following item of thanksgiving and praise,

> I think you will understand when I say that I look back on the last church year with very mixed emotions. The heart attack, which I suffered toward the end of May, had its impact not only in my own personal family, but also in our church family as well. And yet, in spite of the distress of that situation, we are constrained to acknowledge that the mercy of God has been evident in many ways. I will not dwell on the personal aspects of the situation, but just record, to the glory of God, that we have seen the Lord's gracious hand extended to us as a church in a most wonderful way in these days of trial. The unity maintained in the church, the outstanding attendance at the Lord's Day services and the earnest spirit of prayer at the Wednesday

evening meetings have all been matters of great encouragement for which we praise God. I would also like to express in this report, as I have done from the pulpit, my deep gratitude for the love shown to me and to my family by the congregation during these difficult months. It is impossible for me to express to you what this has meant to me.[7]

He stopped preaching in mid-December in preparation for surgery in the New Year. He did share with the congregation, however, a hymn he had written for the Christmas season:

Beneath the sky of Judah's night,
   beneath the special star so bright;
The wonder of the ages see,
   a Saviour born for you and me.

The Angels o'er the manger bend,
   they vainly try to comprehend;
Within the borrowed cradle-stall,
   a new-born babe, but Lord of all.

The shepherds come, the wise men too.
   They gaze in wonder at the view;
The heavenly hosts rejoice to sing
   and draw attention to their King.

Let Christian voices join the praise,
   and celebrate this day of days;
Let God be worshipped and adored,
   for this great gift of Christ the Lord.

On February 22, 1995, Pastor Payne underwent a successful quadruple bypass surgery on his heart. He allowed himself a further two months to recover and returned to lead the Wednesday evening prayer meeting and study on April 26th and began to preach again (once a week only!) on May 14th, almost one full year after his heart attack. It was good to have

---

[7] Trinity Baptist Church, Annual General Business Meeting, Minutes, Oct. 1994.

him back in a preaching and teaching role; it just seemed that all was well with the world once again. At the October business meeting, he began the pastoral report with thanksgiving once again,

> I wish to place on record my gratitude to God for His great mercy in granting success to the operation (Feb 22nd), and for the amazing providential mercies which were evident in so many ways in connection with it....especially, to acknowledge with gratitude the earnest and unceasing prayers offered to God on my behalf by the entire church body...mingled with the prayers of many other Christian friends in many other places.

And, in usual Payne style, closed with an exhortation,

> Complacency is a deadly enemy and will prove detrimental to us; zeal, commitment and spirituality are needed in every Christian committed to this testimony. Let each one examine himself or herself and see whether we have slipped into ruts of spiritual indifference and carelessness, and let us rouse ourselves to follow Christ again more closely and more passionately.

1997 started out much like any other year, with high levels of expectations and the usual array of plans and purposes, both personal and congregational. The words of James, however, were to confront the congregation in a very sudden and powerful way,

> Come now, you who say, "Today or tomorrow we will go into such and such a town and spend a year there and trade and make a profit"—yet you do not know what tomorrow will bring. What is your life? For you are a mist that appears for a little time and then vanishes. Instead you ought to say, "If the Lord wills, we will live and do this or that" (James 4:13–15 ESV).

The Lord's will for Pastor Payne, and for all those who knew and loved him, was that he had but six months left to serve the Lord by serving us.

The pastor is called home

As often as they could, Pastor and Hetty would take their summer holidays at Port Greville, Nova Scotia, on the Bay of Fundy, under the watchful gaze of giant Glooscap, standing guard in nearby Parrsboro. A family friend made a little cottage on a rocky beach available to them and they loved to escape there alone or with members of their family. The quietness and isolation made for a healthy change from the usual routine of busy days and a heavy workload. They enjoyed eating at their favourite local diners and roamed the countryside by car and the waterfront by foot. That summer's outing didn't appear noticeably different from the many trips they had previously made. In Pastor Payne's final sermon at Trinity, the evening of June 15th, he spoke of his anticipation and excitement to be going East for holidays—he even used their previous expeditions on the rocky beach of the Bay of Fundy as a sermon illustration. His sermon was entitled, "Jehovah— the Incomparable God," and his reference was Isaiah 40:9, "Behold your God!" He explained that the answer to the people's problem was to firmly grasp the reality and the glory of their God. He was, first of all, incomparable in His power. To illustrate one way in which this had come home to him personally, he spoke of times he and Hetty had stood on the rocky beach by the cottage, gazing up at the heavens, awestruck by the splendour and glory of the night sky. They pondered, though, how even this magnificence would pale in comparison to the greater glory of God that would one day be revealed. The answer to the question, "Who made these?" was obvious to them both. He went on to speak of God's wisdom, His worthiness and His sovereignty. In making these points clear he quoted King David in 1 Chronicles 29:10–13, some of David's last words before he died,

> Therefore David blessed the Lord before all the assembly; and David said:
>
> "Blessed are You, Lord God of Israel, our Father, forever and ever.
> Yours, O Lord, *is* the greatness,
> The power and the glory,
> The victory and the majesty;
> For all *that is* in heaven and in earth *is Yours*;
> Yours *is* the kingdom, O Lord,

And You are exalted as head over all.
Both riches and honor *come* from You,
And You reign over all.
In Your hand *is* power and might;
In Your hand *it is* to make great
And to give strength to all.

Now therefore, our God,
We thank You
And praise Your glorious name" (NKJV).

The pastor encouraged his listeners to look away from their difficulties and discouragements and "Behold their God!" His final preached words at Trinity, unsurprisingly, were a heartfelt plea to the unsaved to come to Christ.

Everyone wished them well on their trip and looked forward to their return—he always came back energized and full of life. A simple phone call on June 29, 1997, changed that for everyone. Pastor Payne had been called home to be with His Lord on Sunday afternoon. He had been resting at the cottage, awoke, attempted to climb down from the loft and suffered his third and final heart attack. Hetty was there with him at the end. Some in the congregation received the news through phone calls that afternoon, but many didn't hear until they came to church for the evening service. The news hit the people very hard. Details were sparse and Hetty's situation was unclear. They were a long way off, and it would be a few days before plans to deal with necessities could be put in place by the family. Carl was supposed to preach that evening; it was felt a time of prayer would be more beneficial and would allow for the Lord's people to find comfort in God and in one another. The sadness at the people's loss was palpable. However, there was a felt joy in knowing their beloved pastor was at home with the Lord and at peace. Tears were abundant, but they were not, by God's grace, all from sorrow!

For several months the congregation had been preparing for Trinity's twenty-fifth anniversary in October. Pastor Payne, who was always good at planning ahead, had already written "Trinity Baptist Church—Beginnings" which was to be published as part of the anniversary program. In it he said,

> Looking back over twenty-five years it would be sinful if we did not acknowledge that the Lord has done great things for us, and the glory belongs to Him alone. We have been enabled by God's grace to maintain our commitment to the sovereignty of divine grace and the primacy of the preaching of the Word. The congregation has grown slowly but steadily over the years and we have rejoiced to welcome new families and individuals to strengthen our hands in the Lord. People from many different backgrounds have been brought together and yet a good spirit of unity has prevailed for which we must praise God. To say that there have been difficulties and disappointments is to state the obvious and the inevitable! Yet God has blessed the work and we can but praise Him.[8]

He also noted the ongoing desire of the church to be of help and support to other churches.

> We have rejoiced to see other like-minded churches coming into being right here in Ontario and in other parts of Canada and we have enjoyed fraternal ties and fellowship with them. We also rejoice in our participation in the Sovereign Grace Fellowship (SGF) of Churches, which, although very small, does bring us into contact with those of like precious faith. There are churches in other groupings with which we feel, very much, a spiritual unity and whose fellowship is prized. We have been enabled over the years to provide financial assistance to a number of other churches and we rejoice in being able to do so, for this is true fellowship in the gospel.[9]

He closed his brief history with a final note of thanksgiving and praise,

> And what shall we say of the many people who, over the years, have contributed so much to our work here in Trinity. Elders and deacons, Sunday School teachers, youth leaders, children's club helpers, nursery workers, social committee members, those who record and reproduce sermons on tape, treasurers, secretaries; the list could go on. Praise God for all dedicated servants of the Lord who have

---

[8] Trinity Baptist Church, 25th Anniversary Program, 13–14.
[9] Trinity Baptist Church, 25th Anniversary Program, 14–15.

given of their time, talents and energy for the kingdom of God. As we look back over the years, we cannot but praise God from Whom all blessings flow. May He continue to strengthen the work, so that its testimony to the glorious truth of God may continue into the future.[10]

Pastor Payne's funeral service was held at the church on Saturday, July 5, 1997. To allow for the anticipated large number of visitors, seating was arranged downstairs via livestream, as well as a speaker system outside with additional seating under a large tent. As with farewells to all true believers, understanding they simply part from this present world, there was a blend of tears of sorrow and joy. Trinity's loving and much-loved pastor, the founder of the work, was now with the Lord, no longer encumbered with heart issues or concerns of an earthly nature. His time of service among the people was complete and his time of rest and heavenly blessedness had begun.

Not surprisingly, there were several of his favourite hymns sung, including, "Guide Me, O Thou Great Jehovah" and "Loved With Everlasting Love."

Carl Muller, able assistant to the pastor for seven years, led the service. Kirk Wellum, pastor of Sovereign Grace Community Church in Sarnia, who had grown up in Trinity under Pastor Payne's ministry, was invited to preach the message. He spoke on 2 Timothy 4:3: "For the time will come when people will not put up with sound doctrine" (NIV). Long-time friend and compatriot, Brian Robinson, pastor of Faith Baptist Church, Scarborough, offered some reflections on Pastor Payne, the man and the minister. Some of his observations help encapsulate who the people knew this man to really be:

> His gifts were wonderfully used of the Lord as he spoke with great clarity as well as simplicity, making difficult theological concepts plain to even the youngest believers. He loved to exalt Christ, and, as one battered and bruised Christian commented after "accidentally" hearing him preach, "He so preached Christ as the balm of Gilead, that my low-bruised soul wept tears of gladness." A saying for which Bill was well known is "Balance brothers, balance is the key." "He was like the bubble in the middle of the carpenter's level, always at dead

---

[10] Trinity Baptist Church, 25th Anniversary Program, 15.

centre." It was he who gave the Canadian Reformed movement its own distinct flavour, and because of the largeness of his heart, he kept many disparate elements focused on Christ and the task at hand.[11]

There were several passages of Scripture read, but one in particular provided encouragement and comfort to those who would miss the smiling face and deep wisdom of this man. There is coming a day when we will all be together again.

> But I do not want you to be ignorant, brethren, concerning those who have fallen asleep, lest you sorrow as others who have no hope. For if we believe that Jesus died and rose again, even so God will bring with Him those who sleep in Jesus.
>
> For this we say to you by the word of the Lord, that we who are alive *and* remain until the coming of the Lord will by no means precede those who are asleep. For the Lord Himself will descend from heaven with a shout, with the voice of an archangel, and with the trumpet of God. And the dead in Christ will rise first. Then we who are alive *and* remain shall be caught up together with them in the clouds to meet the Lord in the air. And thus we shall always be with the Lord. Therefore comfort one another with these words (1 Thessalonians 4:13–18 NKJV).

Even so, Lord Jesus, come!

Following the funeral there were many opportunities for individuals and groups to reflect on the way God had so ably used Pastor Payne. To help comfort the people of Trinity, a note in the July 6 bulletin read,

> Remember our dear Pastor's family, our church family, our elders and deacons and all those world-wide who mourn Pastor Payne's passing …may we know God's comfort and be given "beauty for ashes, the oil of joy for mourning, the garment of praise for the spirit of heaviness; that (we) may be called trees of righteousness, the planting of the LORD, that He may be glorified" (Isaiah 61:3 NKJV).[12]

---

[11] *Reformation Today* 159 (Sept/Oct 1997): 26.
[12] Trinity Baptist Church, Bulletin, July 6, 1997.

An official note in the board's minutes of July 25 read,

> This is our first meeting since the death of our pastor, William E. Payne. Pastor Payne's faithful, indefatigable, and sacrificial labours have been used of God in the founding and building up of Trinity Baptist Church. The powerful proclamation of the Word has been the hallmark of his ministry amongst us over these 25 years. He will be sorely missed....We need to be supremely confident in the faithfulness of God to supply our every need. We need to work hard to allay fearfulness and anxiety in our people. As we grieve the loss of the pastor, we must not dishonour the Lord by appearing to be faithless in Him.[13]

At the October AGBM, another summation was given, noting the clear hand of God in all he was able to do in the church and around the world,

> The single, solitary event which stands out in our minds as we reflect upon this past year is the homegoing of our pastor, friend, brother, spiritual father, William E. Payne. Words come flooding in as we contemplate our profound loss; we all have our own words and our own stories. But our sense of loss is tempered by his enormous and immeasurable gain. In our more lucid moments, we know that we cannot begrudge him the blessed presence of his Lord. We who remain must be good soldiers of Christ, even as he was...Christ will build His church and further His kingdom. It is in the confidence that this truth engenders that we now press on....May God burn the recent anniversary weekend into our souls, lest we forget what the sovereign God can accomplish through weak vessels, lest we dishonor Him with small faith as we embark upon a journey that will take us to our 50th anniversary.[14]

It is wonderfully ironic that these words came from the heart and pen of Pastor Carl Muller, who would never have imagined, at that point, that the Lord would use him to lead the flock at Trinity along that journey, almost to their fiftieth anniversary!

---

[13] Trinity Baptist Church, board meeting, minutes, July 25, 1997.
[14] Trinity Baptist Church, AGBM, Oct. 1997

Reflections from friends and colleagues flowed in from every quarter, usually referencing a way in which Pastor Payne had touched their lives. Brian Robinson, in the September/October 1997 issue of *Reformation Today*, made the following observations of his dear friend,

> Bill was an able expositor of the Word of God and his people were well grounded in biblical doctrines....Bill was a prodigious worker, reader and writer and was the heart and soul of the Reformed movement in Canada....Bill was, in every way, a pastor's pastor...he had the courage to see that being small was no disgrace and that much of what was done was of a pioneering nature....An oft repeated saying of Bill with regard to his own death: "When they tell you that Pastor Payne is dead, don't believe it. When you hear the news, say to yourself, 'Pastor Payne was never more alive than he is now.'"[15]

In the August 21, 1997, issue of *The Gospel Witness*, one of Pastor Payne's sermons was published, "The Tale of Two Mountains," expounding Hebrews 12:18–24.

> Those who "have come to Mount Zion," that is, those who have put their faith in the Lord Jesus Christ, can expect great things in that realm: glorious wonder, the prevalence of grace and forgiveness, total security, unsurpassable joy, perfection in everything, where God Himself is known.

Again, with a call to repentance and salvation for the lost as he drew the message to a close,

> He is able to save you this morning if you are outside of Christ. He is a mighty Saviour....[And so much so] the author of Hebrews says, "Don't turn back from Him. That is madness. He is such a glorious Saviour. Don't stay away from Him. He is such a magnificent Saviour." Come to Him today and experience something of these glorious blessings of the new covenant as you become a part of it by the grace of God.[16]

---

[15] *Reformation Today* 159 (Sept/Oct 1997): 25–26.
[16] *The Gospel Witness* (August 21, 1997). From a message preached by Pastor Payne at Jarvis Street Baptist Church on Sunday, June 8, 1997.

In that same issue of *The Gospel Witness* there were several personal reflections by those who knew him well. From Geoff Adams, former professor and principal of TBS:

> For many years he [Bill] was a colleague on the Seminary faculty as he lectured on Homiletics and Pastoral Theology. Often have I mentioned that, if I had an opportunity to sit under the ministry of one of our graduates, Bill would be the foremost whom I would select. His ministry was balanced, evangelistic and doctrinal. His influence on other ministers was also seen in his conference ministry and his spearheading the FRPS....We give thanks to our gracious God for such a spiritual gift. He was a beloved friend and we shall miss him greatly.[17]

Roger Fellows, a dear friend in the ministry, noted,

> We do not grieve as those who have no hope, but nevertheless we surely grieve, and rightly so, because a great man and a leader of God's people has been taken from us....It was a joy to work closely with Bill at the pastoral level for about 25 years. There was never a cross word between us. He was a natural leader, but he had a happy knack of making others feel that their contributions were valuable.[18]

Erroll Hulse of England recalled,

> [The founding of Trinity Baptist Church came at a time when] the theological renewal exemplified in the Banner of Truth books was at its height. For Bill and myself, coming into the doctrines of grace involved a deep heart experience. A knowledge of free grace was not just an academic exercise. To Bill these doctrines of grace led to the grace of the doctrines and the arena in which these graces were to be seen in action was the local church.[19]

Though there were reflections and observations by several others, let one final quote provide an essential insight into the character of Pastor Payne. It was highlighted by Thom Smith, a pastoral colleague from West Virginia,

---

[17] *The Gospel Witness* (August 21, 1997).
[18] *The Gospel Witness* (August 21, 1997).
[19] *The Gospel Witness* (August 21, 1997).

But, while Bill was philosophical about his approach to these important matters (preaching and pastoring), he was not stilted, not doctrinaire. There was an ease, a relaxed attitude, which has been all too absent in myself and in many of the Reformed Baptists I had known south of the border. The source of this was not hard to locate: Bill took the things of God utterly seriously, but never took himself so. He was conscientious without the crippling self-consciousness that too often affects reformed-evangelical piety. He was serious without being sour. He was intent without neurotic intenseness. With his grasp of the Gospel firm, he could afford the light touch with other matters. And all this came from the fact that Bill was full of love, love of God and of people, and of the world given by God. This was obvious in his kindness, his gentleness, his seriousness and his humour.[20]

God gifts His church with people necessary for the moment. When their work is done, either big or small, He calls them home to be with Himself and the saints in glory forever. Pastor Payne ran well and finished the race with his eyes fixed on the prize. Any who came within his sphere of influence miss him, though it is unlikely he misses anything in this world, caught up as he is with the glory of God the Father shining upon Him in the face of his Lord and Saviour Jesus Christ.

Twenty-fifth anniversary

Plans for Trinity's twenty-fifth anniversary were in the works for many months prior to October 25–26, 1997. Pastor Earl Blackburn from Los Angeles was the guest speaker at both the Saturday and Sunday services. A buffet lunch was served on Saturday at 1 p.m. in the Park Bible Church gymnasium. About 250 attended to enjoy fellowship, share testimonies and reflections and then remember the first quarter century of church life with a slide show. Dr. Michael Haykin provided copies of a book on the life of Pastor Payne entitled, *William E. Payne: A Memoir*. It contained personal perspectives from family members and others that knew him well. Copies of "Trinity Baptist Church—Beginnings," written beforehand by Pastor Payne, were also made available. This publication covered some of the key events enjoyed by the church over her first twenty-five years of service to God.

---

[20] *The Gospel Witness* (August 21, 1997).

Though somewhat bittersweet, the celebration of God's goodness to the congregation was palpably uplifting and encouraging. Of course, if given the choice, everyone would have preferred to have Pastor Payne there to lead that day and for many more years, but the Lord preferred to have him in glory. However, an awareness of the reality of his standing in the presence of his Lord and Saviour for all eternity, free from physical and earthly issues, allowed joy to exceed sorrow throughout the weekend. After Pastor Payne's death, Hetty found over 100 hymns written by him and tucked away in a file on his desk. With the help of Rachel Thibault (Steenhof), many were set to music and a few of them were introduced and sung as part of the services. His giftedness with poetry was on display and it blended beautifully with his love and skill with music; enjoying the final creation of these hymns was a memorable and honouring means with which to worship the Lord with the heart, mind and soul.

The congregation was given the opportunity to reflect on some aspect of their time at Trinity. Several were published and perhaps sharing a few will suffice to give a sense of how the people felt:

> "Through waves and clouds and storms He gently clears the way." For the last four years we have been coming to Trinity, and every Sunday, as we drive from Ancaster to Burlington, there is joy and gladness in our hearts that we're able to attend Trinity. We are really blessed under the ministry of Pastor Payne, Pastor Muller and many others. The singing of the beautiful hymns with the congregation can be such a blessing in itself. Also, over the years, we've been blessed by the encouragement and prayers from fellow believers when sickness and trials come our way. Yes indeed, we're blessed with a church in the midst of this world. The Lord is in our midst and leads us on (Mary & Walter Kwakernaak).

> Trinity is justly famous for its good preaching, but I always enjoyed the Wednesday evening prayer meetings most. Sunday sermons teach the theory of warfare; Wednesday evenings practice it. And it is on Wednesday evenings that you get to know people. Sometimes you got to know them long before you ever saw them in the flesh; we'd pray for their salvation and, in due course, they'd slip self-consciously into the church. For several months they'd start coming regularly and the

next thing you knew they were helping to collect offering, greeting people at the door, teaching Sunday School, setting up or stacking chairs or frying eggs for a men's breakfast (Peter Pikkert).

Friendships— that is what is best about Trinity. Friendships! (Matt Payne & Jeremy Schofield).

The remembrances of twenty-five years at Trinity Baptist Church is recalling the amazing power and work of the Holy Spirit. We have seen the power of God giving us full measure, pressed down, running over. Together we have seen smooth roads and rough. The faithfulness of God, and the dedication of Reformed teaching of the Word by Pastor Payne gave us constant encouragement and guidance to go on in the strength of the Lord. May the Lord give great grace to those who come after, in preaching and service, to continue this work to the day of Jesus Christ. To God be the glory, great things He has done. Praise the Lord! (Fred & Dorothy Hambides).

Not everyone had opportunity, or even the desire, to verbalize or write down what their Trinity experience meant to them. Much is held within the heart and only known to the individual and to God. Perhaps in glory there will be a complete freedom to share the wonderful ways the Lord taught, equipped and blessed each one.

Getting back on track

The elders (Carl Muller, Colin Wellum, Wilf Ball, Mark Hudson) met on Monday evening, the day after the pastor died. They had to put grief on hold for a time, as the needs of the church family needed to be dealt with. The immediate task facing them was finding speakers to help fill the pulpit for the foreseeable future. Carl agreed to absorb the bulk of the preaching, taking on at least one message a Sunday. Others within the congregation also stepped in to preach and teach and lead. Able men from outside the church were once again looked to for assistance, and they readily offered their time and service. The leadership was often amazed at how men, without any direct planning or contact with one another, were able to cover a range of biblical subject matter resulting in continual spiritual growth and strengthening for the people.

Next, a decision had to be made regarding financial support from the church for Hetty. The matter of a widow's pension would be raised with the deacons at the nearest board meeting. At an appropriate time, Carl met with Hetty to evaluate her situation so recommendations could be brought to the board. The final task was to establish the process through which a new pastor would be considered and evaluated. The elders, acting as pulpit committee, considered a list of several individuals as possibilities over the next few meetings. However, the hearts and minds of at least three of them were continually drawn back to a young man the Lord had already placed in their midst. Pastor Carl Muller had been assisting Pastor Payne for seven years in the areas of teaching, preaching, counselling and visitation. It seemed an unmistakable mercy from God that He had been busy preparing our next pastor right within the church. Pastor Muller was known and loved by the people and, after much prayer and discussion, he was presented at first to the entire board, who endorsed him unanimously. They prepared a contract that would make up part of the presentation to the members for their consideration.

On November 26, 1997, a meeting was held for the membership. It included the full proposal from the board as well as a question and answer time so the members could ask Carl questions. The vote to call him or not was held at a business meeting on December 3rd, where the will of the people was clearly in favour of offering him the role of pastor of Trinity. In stating his willingness to accept the call the church had extended to him, a new phase in the history of the church was about to begin. Perhaps the words of God to Joshua are applicable here,

> After the death of Moses the servant of the Lord, the Lord said to Joshua the son of Nun, Moses' assistant, "Moses my servant is dead. Now therefore arise, go over this Jordan, you and all this people, into the land that I am giving to them, to the people of Israel" (Joshua 1:1–2 ESV).

Moses had been used by God to lead His people out of Egypt and to the border of the promised land. Now, he had died, but there was no time to waste; there were many important tasks to be accomplished and the people needed a new leader. There can be little doubt that Joshua was mildly terrified. Three times in this first chapter the Lord encourages him and tells him not to fear. The Lord also gave him the grounds for that courage.

"Just as I was with Moses, so I will be with you. I will not leave you or forsake you. Be strong and courageous" (Joshua 1:5–6 ESV).

The elders encouraged their new pastor with similar words and exhortations. All were agreed on the faithfulness of God in the care of His people and the fact that He could and would equip him as needed!

As in the case of a Joshua following a Moses, one of the greatest challenges that can face a new pastor is trying to live and serve in the shadow of the former pastor, especially a founding pastor and one who had served faithfully for twenty-five years. Pastor Muller had a taste of that in the time he ministered at Fundamental Baptist Church (now Bath Road Baptist) in Kingston; a situation in which he followed another long-serving, much-loved and respected founding pastor, Sam Dempster. He experienced some distinct challenges in that situation and his memory of those times was still fresh in his mind. Taking the lead at Trinity at this time was not a situation Pastor Muller would have chosen for himself, but he was prayerfully submissive to the guidance of the Holy Spirit. He and Heather agreed to heed the call to Trinity's pastorate at the recommendation of the board and with the support of the members, but also with some residual fear and trembling.

Some background on Pastor Muller

It helps to get accurate information from a primary source. Carl wrote a brief testimony for the March 1998 *Trinity Times*, just a month or so into his pastorate. He briefly highlights his journey to that point:

> I was born in South Africa and lived there until I was twelve years old, at which point my parents decided that they had had enough of the apartheid situation. We immigrated to North America and lived in California (for 9 sunny months), Toronto (where we saw snow for the first time) and then settled in Burlington where my parents still live. I was 17 and in Grade 11 when I was converted through the bold witness of fellow students who invited me to attend church with them at the (then) Brant Street Bible Church. During my last year of high school I had the vague notions of some kind of ministry, and this led to studies at Ontario Bible College.
>
> During my time at OBC, in the late seventies, I began attending Trinity where, under Pastor Payne's rich ministry, I began to get

a better grip on Reformed teaching. In 1980, after graduating from OBC, I moved to Waterloo where I did a degree in history at the University of Waterloo. At the same time I was the pastor of Blair Baptist Church where the Lord's people lovingly bore with a very green and inexperienced young man. In 1985, I was called to the (then) Fundamental Baptist Church in Kingston. Within the space of that one year I moved to Kingston, married Heather, was ordained and found out that we were expecting Jessica.

In 1989 we moved back to this area and was once again under Pastor Payne's ministry, with the added privilege of working alongside him and the other men on the board. God's leading to the point at which we find ourselves today has been clear and unmistakable, for which we are thankful. I am excited about the work God has for me here and the privilege of ministering among people whom I know and feel to be my brothers and sisters in Christ, and whom I love dearly in the Lord.[21]

Carl and Heather stepped out in faith, with a sincere desire to honour the Lord's leading in their lives and to serve in whatever manner He chose. The people of Trinity were thrilled to have him as pastor and were ready to support him in the ministry. There were commitments to pray for him as he began to walk the path initially forged by God through the efforts and work of Pastor Payne. In the early days it was difficult not to think of what Pastor Payne would do or say in any given situation. His echo was often heard in the minds and hearts of the people, Carl's included, though not in a negative or restrictive way. His love for the Lord's work and for the Lord's people was a blessed memory that would, over time, fade somewhat in volume, but never in clarity.

At the helm

Perhaps it was the upcoming new millennium or just a new generation arising, but the greater formalism of that previous age shifted to a greater familiarism when addressing the pastor and his wife. It seemed it was often Pastor and Mrs. Payne, whereas at this time it was more often heard to be Carl and Heather—somewhat parallel to what would become the common usage of Kate and William where no one would address Queen Elizabeth

---

[21] Trinity Baptist Church, *Trinity Times*, March 1998.

Coming of age 89

Carl & Heather Muller

and Prince Philip as Liz and Phil. He was understood to be Pastor Muller but comfortably answered to Carl or pastor Carl and will generally be referred to in that manner throughout the rest of this history.

On January 25, 1998, Hugh Gordon, missionary to Pakistan for many years, was invited to bring a message and a charge to Carl and to the congregation as he formally took up his duties. Hugh preached on 2 Peter 1:2–11. Part of his charge to the pastor read,

> Using the analogy of a chef preparing a meal, the minister's obligation is to prepare the ministry of the Word of God in such a way that it feeds his own soul. When he comes into the pulpit, he has burning in his heart a devotion to Jesus Christ, so that he lays before the congregation a feast of which he, himself, has already tasted deeply. May you become such a minister, brother, having been wrought upon by the Holy Spirit, first taste then break the bread, the Word of God. May you be so ravished by the glories of Christ in your own heart and soul in the privacy of your own study, that you come to the pulpit to set before the people the kind of fare that will cause God's people to hunger more and more after Him.

Casting his gaze on the congregation he continued,

> May God enable you, pastor, elders, congregation, to be the kind of people that are not only Christian but are seen in every area of your lives to truly magnify the Lord Jesus Christ in this community.... Read 2 Peter 1:5–10 and ask the Holy Spirit to burn these verses into your hearts. Go home and fall on your knees and pray, "God, I will not rest until You make me this kind of Christian." As a congregation, do not rest until God is working this way in your lives. Then commit yourselves to prayer for your pastor as he takes up his responsibilities, so that from this pulpit, Sunday by Sunday, you will be fed. Pray you will be found a willing people as He leads you on in the day of His power and in the day of His triumph. Those who are strangers to grace will so see the glory of Christ, the love of Christ and the power of Christ working in everyday areas of your lives, that they will begin to clamour after Christ themselves.[22]

---

[22] Trinity Baptist Church, *Trinity Times*, March 1998.

The following Sunday, February 2, 1998, Carl Muller, formerly assistant to Pastor Payne, began his official duties as the new pastor of Trinity Baptist Church.

In the "Elder's Report" for the October 1998 business meeting, about eight months after beginning his official duties, Carl presented two words on which the congregation was to reflect in the upcoming year: *Change* and *Challenge*. He referred to the significant changes that had occurred over the past year: new pastoral leadership, the many men who had ministered in evening service from July 1997 to February 1998 and the new leadership arising in several of the church ministries. However, to encourage the people he wrote,

> Yet through it all, what buoys the hearts of God's people is the fact that the Lord does not change. We have been blessed with His presence, this demonstration of His power, with blessings which have encouraged and strengthened. Through it all, we have known an encouraging measure of unity and peace. Through it all we have felt the same sense of purpose and mandate: namely, to glorify God, to proclaim His Word, to build up the body, to grow in holiness, to win the lost! And through it all, the Lord has given faith, strength and grace to equip us for the tasks He sets before us.[23]

He went on to address the challenges the people faced as a congregation: adjusting to a new pastor who is not Bill Payne, seeing and addressing the work that needed to be done, both at Trinity, within the SGF and the wider world. He summed these up,

> In light of these changes, and in the face of these challenges, let humble, fervent prayer be the order of the day—prayer for the leadership, for spiritual growth, for divine direction and wisdom, for love and unity, for merciful provision. And we shall watch for the return of prayers, and "look to see what He will say" to us, and what He will do through us.[24]

---

[23] Trinity Baptist Church, AGBM, "Elder's Report," Oct. 1998.
[24] Trinity Baptist Church, AGBM, "Elder's Report," Oct. 1998.

This was the basis on which he was looking to guide Trinity during his mandate. We are to look to the Lord first and foremost, and serve Him with heart and soul and strength and mind, as His workmanship in Christ.

To build or not to build

Ever since the idea of purchasing land was first raised, the hope was that, someday, a new addition could be built to create the much-needed space for seating, fellowship and classes. Plans for adding a new auditorium of some sort had been in the works for several years. The land sale had been conditional on Trinity receiving approval to build on its present site, which had been granted in principle. With the decade drawing to a close, and the seating space starting to shrink once again, the board decided to propose a building plan to the congregation. They knew that a sizeable monetary gift was coming from the sale of a church Trinity had supported in London; the size of the gift was, at this point, still unknown. With plans to seat about 350, the initial cost estimate was around $600,000. The board would recommend to the people to target having $400,000 on hand before breaking ground, and then look to the Lord and the generosity of people in special offerings for the balance. The board felt it had done its due diligence in terms of pricing and planning and were excited to hear what the members thought.

The proposal was presented to them at the February 1999 business meeting; they were asked to prayerfully consider it and come back with questions. At the follow up meeting on March 3rd, a time of questions and answers was held in which two or three key issues were raised that some felt pointed to potential weaknesses in the board's economic analysis of the build. Arguments were met with counterarguments and, though a good spirit overruled the proceedings, in the end there was insufficient support to see the plans move forward. The board would go back and rethink and reshape their plans and proposals. It would require a new millennium before the next proposal would go forward. Fortunately, that was right around the corner.

5

A time of expansion

The 2000s

◇◇◇◇◇◇◇◇

The new millennium

The world must have been greatly relieved to watch the clock tick past midnight, marking the end to the 1900s, and not grind to a devastating halt as the 2000s got underway. Those to the West had the advantage of watching those in the first time zones away to the East encounter—and survive—the Y2K threat without any notable fallout. No doubt, there were many disappointed alarmists; the expected chaos would have to wait to be initiated by more mundane crises. Most generations have witnessed the rollover of the centuries, but few have had the privilege to live in two different millennial eras. Once the initial thrill of that privilege had worn off, however, most people just went to bed and got some sleep. Perhaps, after waking on the morning of January 1st some of the biggest and best resolutions ever were made; as always, just not sure how many had been rescinded by the 2nd.

The long-awaited build

With the defeat of the board's building proposal the previous year, the elders and deacons went back to the planning stage to reevaluate the areas of congregational concern that needed to be addressed. Everyone was still on board with building, but the financial issues had to be tightened. The Lord helped provide resolution to this through another church's generosity. In January, Trinity received a financial gift from the sale of a sister work in London, Westminster Baptist. This work had been pastored for many years by Brian Robinson, but he had been called to another work in Scarborough and the church in London was closing their doors. Trinity had helped support the London work for several years and, with the sale of the property, a part of the funds from the sale, about $155,000, was graciously given to Trinity. Portions of this gift were directed to two projects: $10,000 went to help purchase a much-needed vehicle for Pastor Robinson, $12,000 went to support Pilgrim Baptist Fellowship in Ancaster. There was some scattered questions within the SGF as to the purpose of this gift and how broadly it should be used. To clarify, a letter was sent from Trinity to the SGF pastors which read, in part,

> We understand that there has been some confusion over the past eighteen months with respect to this gift, its purpose and its mode of distribution. Since no-one within the SGF had direct contact with the final decisions of the Westminster congregation, at least with respect to details regarding the gift, and no specific instructions subsequently came with the gift, Trinity must take responsibility for its use.[1]

The balance, about $133,000, was added to Trinity's building fund begun several years prior. This gift was certainly an answer to prayer and helped the board move a step closer to recommending, once again, the pursuit of a new building. The board, though interested in the build, was just as determined not to allow it to become the sole target of the Lord's

---

[1] Trinity Baptist Church, letter from the elders to the SGF pastors, 2000.

goodness and the faithfulness of God's people in their giving. Eventually, several financial gifts (totalling about $51,000) went to help with specific needs of two missionary couples, as well as a new church plant in Toronto.

Early in 2001, a detailed discussion about building became a central focus of the board once again. A new proposal was brought to the members, but this time they were asked to approve the exploration of solutions to the space issues related to seating and classrooms. A broad financial framework, without timelines or specific dollar amounts, was presented and accepted by them. It was agreed, in principle, that, until a specific financial goal of saving had been reached, there would be no movement on construction. Various building proposals would be explored by the board and, once agreement had been reached, a recommendation with the necessary details would be brought to the members for discussion. Even as late as October, however, there was still ongoing discussion related to the various options. Questions were being asked about how big was too big and if a church plant would be a better alternative. These questions were similar to those asked by board members back when deciding to buy the property across No. 2 SR. Now, however, there were new people on the board who had not been part of those conversations and old ground had to be reworked for their benefit and to their satisfaction. This process was helpful in realigning priorities and preparing for questions from the membership.

Finally, in January 2001, the elders and deacons had produced a summary that laid out again the five possible courses of action:

1. Make no changes at all.
2. Increase the current auditorium capacity to its max.
3. Build a new addition.
4. Buy another building.
5. Plant a new work.

Weighing the pros and cons of each position eventually led the board to (once again) unanimously decide to stay put and expand on the present site. At about the same time, ideas were floated regarding the revamping of classroom and storage space in the basement of the old building. This area had a very tired and worn look to it and needed a significant makeover. Thus, the board prepared to recommend Option 3 to the congregation with the best supporting rationale and argument possible. The proposal would include timelines and estimated total costs.

Over two board meetings in February 2001, the financing details were pieced together. The total cost of the project would now be about $900,000. The church had about $200,000 on hand and could probably carry a debt load of about $3,000 per month. A target of $600,000 on hand was to be reached before a shovel went in the ground; the balance would be taken out in some sort of loan. There were lots of excellent questions from some board members that were, fortunately, followed by some well thought out answers from others. There were unknowns that also had to be explored:

- What strain would long term debt financing place on other church commitments?
- What would be an appropriate ratio of loan/cash on hand?
- How much buffer should be built into the estimates?
- Should private money from people outside the church be pursued?
- How much could the church borrow and would a bank offer a mortgage?
- What other means could be used to raise the outstanding funds?

These were serious questions that needed to be answered before bringing the proposal to the people. Because of the complexities involved, the board decided to simply announce the general plan for the package in February to get the people thinking and praying about the best course of action; a final plan would be presented a month or so later. This would allow the board time to firm up many of the finer details and be ready to answer any questions that might arise. This was not something to be rushed

At the business meeting in mid-April, the big decision was made, in principle, to proceed with the plan to build an addition on to the present church building. Even though this transpired with a simple vote, it was really the culmination of many months of discussion, debate, deliberation and investigation. With about $200,000 in the bank, acquiring the additional $400,000 needed to begin the project began with a special offering in late May and early June. Pledges for gifts were also received with the intent of seeing them fulfilled by the beginning of the build. Estimated costs of building materials and actual construction were also being tracked down. If all the finances did not come in on time, the work would be scaled back accordingly, such as finishing the balcony at a later date. By the end of the summer, about $230,000 had been given or pledged. By the end of 2001, after a second special offering in late September, there was still a shortfall of about $140,000. The board, in examining the possibility of a fundraising campaign, brought in an expert in the area who offered a very thorough presentation at a board meeting. However, when the discussions ended, there was strong consensus the church should stick to free will offerings by the people within the church as being the most biblical approach, and the one displaying the greatest faith in the Lord to provide, as He always had!

In February 2002, detailed planning for the build picked up steam. Seeking out loans at decent rates from banks or other sources was pursued by the treasurer. An architect was commissioned to create a set of drawings so "real costs" could be viewed rather than vague estimates. A building committee was formed to make recommendations on what work could be phased in over time (perhaps postpone the kitchen, washrooms and renovations to the older building).

In May, Joe VandeMerwe was appointed as project manager. He would have the key role in booking the necessary tradespeople and keeping the project as much on time and within budget as possible. By June, the church had received approval to extend the timeframe previously granted for the site plan, and applications were being submitted for the required permits. The project would begin with the septic system which would be relocated to the north end of the new parking area across No. 2 SR.

In Fall 2002, the congregation was informed that, as is often the case with construction projects, a series of issues would delay the beginning of the build until Spring 2003. In the meantime, building permits began to arrive, the design of the balcony was finalized and the fire department's requirement of 100 m^3 of water on site would be met with two buried tanks under a portion of the land north of No. 2 SR. To provide greater water service to the property, a well was dug and a source of water discovered. Unfortunately, the flow was low, at about 2 litres per minute. It was sufficient to build up the water needed for a weekend service, but not enough to meet fire regulations to protect the building in case of fire. The congregation was kept up to date with the timelines and financial progress through letters and membership meetings.

As in the past, the congregational giving toward the special needs of the build was outstanding. By February 2003, all the necessary funds to start ($600,000) were either in hand through gifts or near-at-hand through pledges. The membership voted to go ahead and start the building process as soon as frost was out of the ground. That day came on Saturday, March 15, 2003, when a groundbreaking ceremony took place for the new addition.

A note recording the event was included in the May 16th bulletin,

> New beginnings! About 80 people, including Burlington's deputy mayor, gathered as the sun beamed down yesterday to witness the start of a new building for our church (or did they all gather to witness our pastor climbing up into a front end loader that had been parked on the side lawn for a photo op?). The disbelieving will be able to see for themselves in the paper. The crowd stood around Carl, the deputy mayor and Joe VandeMerwe. Carl spoke of causes for praising God in bringing us to the point where we can build and expressed the desire to see the new facility bring glory to God. Jeroon VandeMerwe read Psalm 103 and Doc Wellum led in prayer. Following that, the deputy mayor spoke for a few minutes to congratulate the congregation on this venture and expressed her confidence that we'd see good things in days ahead.[2]

The project was no longer a mere hope or conjecture, it was actually underway. Jeroon VandeMerwe became the board liaison with the project manager. With the usual ebb and flow associated with these large projects, construction continued through the summer and fall and then through the following winter and spring. Tours of the partially finished structure gave the congregation some appreciation of its size and layout. Week by week, the new changes were noted and applauded. Windows, shingles, bricking and stonework, all added to the expectation that 2004 would be the year of completion! Even in these latter stages, there were numerous details to be worked out and decided upon: style of pews or selection of chairs, new piano and organ, types of flooring, style of washroom fixtures, countertops, the set-up of the kitchen, the hanging of doors, making drinking water available, adequate sound equipment, carpets, railings, elevator, colour schemes, to name just a few. These were each handled in turn under the specific oversight of Jeroon and the building committee.

When costing finally became a firm reality it was apparent that additional funding would be needed to complete the work. In February 2004, the members were told an additional $100,000 would have to be raised. There was a positive response once again and by the time the doors were ready to open, all the finances were well in hand.

---

[2] Trinity Baptist Church, Bulletin, May 16, 2003.

A time of expansion 99

Trinity Baptist Church, Burlington, Ont., July 2004
Photo © Henry van Zanden

Finally, on Sunday, June 13, 2004, the doors were opened, and the Trinity Baptist Church family enjoyed their first service in the new addition. There was also the added blessing of the inaugural messages being delivered by Dr. D.A. Carson, whose aunt, Maureen Foster, was a church member.

The church did not hold an official dedication ceremony for the building until the fall, when, on Saturday, September 11, 2004, special meetings were held for just that occasion. A fellowship hour took place at 6 p.m., followed by a dedication of the building. This was the Lord's building for His work and to be used as He saw fit. Pastor Kirk Wellum preached a message in which the grace and mercy of God was paramount. Pastor Brian Robinson, longtime friend of Trinity preached on Sunday. Through it all, the congregation rejoiced in God's wonderful provision and providential oversight in bringing all the details of the work together. Pastor Payne would have been pleased to see that his recommendation to pursue land to prepare for possible expansion sixteen years earlier had reached its fulfillment in this new and exciting way!

Not done yet

The building expansion involved more than just the new addition. It would also include a renovation of the classroom spaces beneath the old auditorium, the connector area between the new and the old, as well as the completion of the work on the balcony. Late in the year, a plan was formulated by the board to cover both the financial and construction details of this next phase. Early estimates put the total cost of these final parts of the project somewhere between $150,000 and $200,000. The plans were discussed at each of the board meetings throughout the spring and fall. The work would involve renovation to both the upper and lower levels of the old building. Changes would have to be made to the roof, one stairwell and certain storage areas. The lower level would be dedicated primarily to classrooms, whereas the upper level would be mostly nursery. The pews in the old auditorium would be sold and replaced with chairs. The ability to rearrange the space with chairs and tables allowed for greater flexibility of use. A new structure for the church library would be designed and included in the renovation.

In November 2006, a letter was distributed to the members with details of the work and its estimated cost, which was now about $225,000. There was, therefore, a building fund to fill before the work could begin. Due to a variety of other priorities, this work would not be completed until early 2009; the old auditorium, newly painted and carpeted, began to be used in the New Year, and the classrooms downstairs were in use by May, much to the delight of the various classes who all had their own space, along with the novelty of a larger shared space for corporate singing. For now, the building and renovation work was complete. The facility was as up-to-date and functional as could be. The Lord was to be praised for once again displaying the faithfulness of a loving, heavenly Father.

Planting a church

One of the overarching desires of a church is to see the gospel of the Lord Jesus Christ spread beyond its own limited borders. A biblical means to that end involves the planting of additional churches in locations where the gospel is scarce or non-existent. The idea of planting a work had been discussed in a hypothetical manner among the elders in the past, but no concrete steps had yet been taken in pursuing that kind of project. That changed when, in Spring 2002, a few families approached the elders expressing their interest and desire to see a work started in the town of Grimsby. They had formed a regional prayer meeting group in that area and had made the possibility of beginning a work there a specific and earnest matter of prayer. It weighed so much on their hearts they decided to step forward, lay out their desires before the elders and see where the Lord might lead. Their plan was to continue to have regional prayer meetings there and see what kind of broader interest might be aroused. The elders agreed and, as a matter of spiritual oversight, one elder would join them on a rotating monthly basis. Elder Wilf Ball offered to work closely with these brothers and sisters as they sought the Lord's will in this endeavour. This program continued over the next couple of years.

During that time, the people meeting in Grimsby began to formulate a plan for meetings and a timeline for a possible church plant. In November 2004, Wilf distributed to the elders a five-page proposal for planting an official work in Grimsby. In the absence of an official playbook to follow in terms of church planting, it was an excellent starting point for what could or should be done in this particular instance. The proposal included a general introduction delineating the rationale for a church plant at this time. It also identified some of the necessary resources that would be need to be explored: financial options, beginning with giving by the first attending families; potential financial help from Trinity and the SGF; availability of personnel and how their gifts could be incorporated into the planting of a church. The official proposal read,

> It is proposed that early in 2005, a satellite work of TBC be initiated in or near the town of Grimsby. In its initial "Start-up" phase, this venture would begin meeting once per Sunday on its own in a rented hall or school gymnasium. At this point, the elders do not have a consensus as to whether starting with a morning or evening service would be the preferred approach. That decision would come in consultation with the group itself.

The proposal also included extensive details on how the work would function (as a ministry of TBC) and how it would be phased in over time: start-up, organizing, developing a constitution. The mode, goals and objectives of each phase were clearly laid out and showed a depth of careful thought and planning. It required three conditions to start:

1. Enthusiastic commitment to this proposal by the group in Grimsby and by the board of Trinity Baptist Church.
2. Acceptance of this, or any proposal put forward, by the congregation of Trinity Baptist Church.
3. Financial means at hand to meet the start-up phase requirements.

Though major steps were not taken in early 2005, the seeds had been planted and the watering begun. Over the next year or so, representatives from Grimsby met with the elders to discuss progress and challenges, along with answering key questions. To the people eager to get the plant going, the progress must have seemed slow at times. In October 2006, representatives from Grimsby again met with the elders to see if things could move ahead more rapidly. They were now meeting on Wednesday evenings in the Carnegie Hall Library building in Grimsby, their first foray out of people's homes and more into the public square. They understood they were not yet ready to expand on the work, but they were looking for a timeframe in which they could move in that direction. The elders laid out their reasons for caution and patience. This was a new frontier for everyone involved and there was the potential to encounter hazards that had not yet been anticipated. That being said, the time seemed ripe for more definitive steps.

One step was to help formulate a roster of speakers to help them out on Wednesday evenings. In November 2006, the Grimsby representatives again met with the elders and began to go back over the church planting proposal presented on their behalf back in October 2004. They hoped to begin Sunday evening services soon, but planned to join with Trinity for the Lord's table after the morning service each month. Moving the Lord's table to the morning service, when this started in May, facilitated their participation.

In January 2007, the Trinity Baptist Church eldership proposed they assume official oversight of the Grimsby church plant. To help with finances, $3,000 was set aside for advertising, signs, a website and other start-up expenses. This proposal was passed by the members of Trinity in February. Trinity's treasurer began to keep a set of parallel accounts for the Grimsby work to assist in the transition, and until they received their own charitable status from the government. Offerings collected by them were set aside for their use. A slate of speakers was set up to fill their pulpit on Sunday evenings. Several men were used in this capacity, with the services organized and led by the men from Grimsby. It was a smooth start to what everyone hoped would be a long ministry.

In January 2008, elder Wilf Ball updated the elders on the development of the work. His efforts as a liaison to the elders and as a spiritual leader for the congregation was appreciated by everyone in both groups. It was encouraging to see the number of attendees growing, along with very faithful support from the core group. In fact, with the rate of growth, the library facility was soon too small to hold them all. There was discussion, even at that early stage, of soon moving to a morning service. That planning would depend very much on what facilities might be available to them.

One practical concern from Trinity's perspective was the overall financial impact on offerings when the funds dedicated to the Grimsby work were removed from Trinity's budget. It was possible there could be a 10 to 15 per cent drop in giving as plans moved forward. The board cheerfully committed that concern to the Lord and He, ever the faithful One, enabled the congregation to more than make up for the lost revenue.

By April, a copy of Grimsby's proposed constitution was distributed for discussion and feedback. It had been well prepared and there was little to amend. At this time, with his willing consent, elder Wilf Ball was nominated to act as elder at Grimsby for an initial twelve-month period. Others from within the congregation would be added to create a leadership team to guide them through the opening stages of the development of the work. Then, on the evening of Sunday, April 15, 2008, the initial service of Grimsby Bible Church was held in the Grimsby library. It was a day of high celebration and great thankfulness to God for His mercy and for the many men and women who had laboured diligently for this milestone. This would be their home base until they moved into their own church building almost five years later.

On June 25, 2008, eighteen members from Trinity became the founding members of the newly formed Grimsby Bible Church. They formally accepted their new constitution and applied for their charitable status, which was granted in 2010. They planned to continue with evening services and weekly prayer meetings until the fall when morning services would begin, the first being held on September 28. A commissioning service for the members leaving for Grimsby took place at the last morning service in August. It was a bittersweet moment, as most of those founding members had grown up at Trinity, had family and friends at Trinity and had laboured faithfully for the Lord and fellow members at Trinity for many years. The Lord, however, was continuing to build His church. The Grimsby area would now have an additional outlet for the proclamation of the gospel of the Lord Jesus Christ.

It was not long before a potential pastor was introduced to the congregation. By the start of 2009, David Ens, who had several years of pastoral experience, began to do some preaching at Grimsby and he and his family seemed to be fitting in very well. In April the congregation gladly received into formal leadership their first two elders, Wilf Ball and David Ens, along with two deacons, Rick Thibault and Joel Thibault. Pastor Carl and some of the elders from Trinity attended their service on April 19, 2009, to dedicate these men to the Lord as the first official board of Grimsby Bible Church. In May, David was taken on as a summer intern and in the fall ministered part-time while pursuing his studies at TBS. In January 2010, the congregation formally voted David to the pastoral position, though he didn't begin full-time work until after graduation. So, on May 9, 2010, he took on the full load of pastoral responsibilities at Grimsby. They were now fully operational and ready to be used in the service of the Lord.

This, of course, did not mark the end of the relationship between the two churches. In early 2010, Trinity offered to give Grimsby the piano that was downstairs in the fellowship hall. It seemed appropriate that this piano, which had been donated to Trinity by Eloise Meikle, should be moved to help with worship at Grimsby where Eloise's daughter Jackie Ball and her family were now members. Then, in February 2012, Trinity sent a gift of $20,000 to help with the purchase of an Anglican church building that had become available in town. This helped give the congregation a more distinct presence in the community of Grimsby and a facility they could shape and use as they sought to shine the light of the gospel into their neighbourhood.

The newly organized Sovereign Grace Fellowship of Canada

Back in the early 1970s, when publicly identifying as a Reformed Baptist was in its infancy in Ontario and the rest of Canada, Pastor Payne was at the forefront of connecting men who shared a set of common Reformed beliefs. At the heart was a biblical understanding of the sovereignty of God, particularly as it related to salvation. Being an avowed Calvinist was not well received in the broader evangelical world at the time, but a small group of like-minded men began to meet to discuss pertinent theological issues and band together for support and encouragement. Through monthly fellowship meetings, retreats and conferences these men promoted the key precepts of this worldview, especially by promoting the reading of newly published literature bringing the light and insights of the Reformers to the forefront once again. This fellowship of Sovereign Grace pastors was always a relatively loose network connecting men and churches of common belief around the Word. At the turn of the millennium, however, a group of these Reformed pastors got together and sought to bring a greater level of structure and coherence to the fellowship.

In October 2000, the Trinity board began to examine and discuss the constitutional proposal distributed by the organizing committee of the SGF. It was hoped Trinity could be a founding member of this newly established fellowship. Could the church commit to its purpose and its governing principles? Some of the men had experienced the pluses and minuses of overarching church organizations in other settings, and not all comments were initially favourable to the idea. Questions arose in key areas, such as the legal parameters of property ownership and financial oversight. However, the central area of concern had to do with putting the autonomy of the local church at risk. Would the SGF ever be in a position to tell the local church what it should or shouldn't do and exercise authority in doing so? These questions, and others, were discussed and debated at length at board meetings over the next several months.

By February 2001, legal counsel had assured the board that there was nothing in the proposed constitution that posed any threat to the areas in question. If anything untoward were to arise, and no adequate solution found, the church could opt out of membership at any time of its own choosing, without any further obligation or commitments. It was agreed then to bring it to the members as soon as the building proposal had been presented to them. In March, a copy of the SGF constitution was distributed to the members; they were asked to read it and bring any questions to a member's meeting set for the 28th of that month. The presentation by the elders was well-received and so, at a business meeting on May 9, 2001, the members approved the submission of an official request to join the SGF. The application was gladly accepted and Trinity formally came into membership shortly thereafter.[3]

There has been a good relationship between Trinity and her sister churches in the SGF ever since. Trinity has been blessed through pastoral pulpit exchanges, the hosting of two Annual General Assemblies, Pastor Muller serving on the Board of Directors on more than one occasion and the opportunity for a Trinity elder to fill the role of SGF administrative coordinator for a twelve-year period. Some members have served in an organizational capacity for special SGF events that have been a blessing to a whole host of families from the other churches; just as others have done for the benefit of Trinity as well! At various times and in various ways, Trinity has also helped out member churches financially, and by sending men to preach when needed, sharing facilities for special events, offering spiritual counsel when asked, lending musicians to help play for their services and sharing in mission projects and missionary work. Perhaps the most significant means of help, however, would be the prayer support offered on a regular basis. Many people in Trinity knew individuals and families in other SGF churches and prayed for them when needs arose, or just generally in an ongoing manner. It was that network of prayerful brothers and sisters that has, without a doubt, benefitted the member churches of the SGF the most. May this always be the case, to the glory of God!

---

[3] See https://www.sgfcanada.com/about-us#history to read more about the SGFs founding.

Insight for Life Seminars

Evangelical churches are always on the lookout for effective ways to reach deeper into their local communities. Because of Trinity's location in the country, there is little or no foot traffic past the church and most cars go by so fast they often just glance on the way to or from work and perhaps catch the name on the sign. It is important to find channels through which the world outside can be met face to face. Some efforts had been made to canvas the newly built neighbourhoods bounded by Appleby Line, Walkers Line, the 407 and Dundas Street. Several distributions of literature, including invitations to special events at the church, were made over the years, though there was very little response. One of the elders floated the idea of a public presentation on a topic of general interest, but offered with a biblical perspective from a Christian worldview. All agreed the idea had merit and should be pursued. An intriguing and appropriate name was required. After several suggestions fell flat, the name Insight for Life (IFL) seminar was adopted.

There were logistical and content related issues to be dealt with. A central location would be required, so a room seating at least a hundred people was located and booked at the Burlington Public Library. A brochure was created to advertise this event, along with posters and informative ads for the local papers. A list of possible topics and speakers was soon established. Finally, on September 25, 2008, the first seminar was presented. Pastor Muller dealt with the wide-ranging topic of marriage. There were fewer in attendance than hoped, but, thankfully, there was a small number of people who could claim to be "not from Trinity."

In spite of the small numbers, other IFL seminars were held over the next couple of years. Dr. Steve Swallow spoke on depression, and elder Jonathan Wellum spoke on financial stewardship. The purpose was to educate individuals as to what the Bible taught on these serious and relevant topics. And, the gospel was always proclaimed. Even though follow-up seminars covered issues such as effective parenting, health and well-being, and financial stewardship, the numbers never exceeded about thirty-five in attendance each time. It was a little discouraging, but certainly worthwhile for those who came. With the apparently low impact on the community at large, it was felt that the seminars should be put on hold for the time being and other forms of outreach pursued.

Children's talks

At one point in his ministry, Pastor Payne presented a series of talks directed specifically to the children. His love for the younger generation was evident through his successful efforts to apply biblical truth to the world in which kids lived by using images and language that was easily understood. They would be quite excited when he stepped to the side of the pulpit and shared an anecdote or a photo or simply an account of some familiar aspect of God's world. He showed the same compassion and grasp of a young heart as he and Hetty did in their many years of service with the Kids Club program. These talks were not a regular part of his ministry but emerged periodically over the years.

On January 12, 2003, a new storyteller emerged with a similar desire to reach out to some of the youngest hearts and minds in the congregation. Elder Gord Vander Pol asked for permission to resurrect the children's talks. He had a burden for the souls of these young children, and he wanted to play a part in making their special needs a matter of regular ministry within the church service.

Fortunately, Gord Vander Pol had some warm-up sessions as Sunday School superintendent before taking on these talks. For example, in September, as a traditional and transitional kick-off to the new year, all the classes would meet as a single group before kids went off with their respective teachers. It seemed appropriate to present an important object lesson to the assembled Sunday School—an overall challenge for the coming year. A couple of these lessons have been burned into the memories of those present and have become part of Trinity lore. No-one could forget the flattened cat carcass in the pizza box (which had been stored at his house for some time prior) or the unexpected shock of the hammer slamming down on the lovely little toy train as it quietly chugged its way around the track. Not all sessions involved such dramatic flair, but it was always a possibility!

In the talks in the service, there was always a biblical theme and part of the challenge was to listen carefully to the story or account and anticipate what lesson was coming. There was great variety and creativity in terms of topics, some of which ran as a series for many weeks. For example: bears, human heads, colours, being lost, sports, toys, pigs, fruit, sheep, chocolate bars, feet, the letter "T", words that go forward and back, cats, time, trees and rodents. He was not afraid to share events from his own life; this usually involved the learning of his own lessons, often the hard way. There was a little something for everyone!

At least five characteristics became regular and expected elements of the talk. Mr. VanderPol would: (1) wear a tie that matched his topic; (2) call up a volunteer (or two or three), usually asking if there was anyone who had never been called up before; (3) hand over an object pertinent to the talk to be held up high so everyone could see; (4) weave a story of the object to a biblical theme or lesson; (5) close off saying, "And with that, let us pray." In the talks themselves, he would often plead with the children to believe in Jesus and be saved, and in the prayers that closed the talks he would again plead with the Lord to enable those children to believe in Jesus and be saved. He had a very focused mission in mind! There were, of course, many other important lessons for the children, but in each of them it was evident to everyone that the love of God was on display in the love of that storyteller.

Policies

Every so often it is good to look back over policies or documents from previous years and ensure they are up to date. Over a three-year period, the elders re-examined the church constitution and by-laws and recommended to the church several modifications. These were not substantive in terms of core content, but eliminated some inconsistencies, clarified some procedures that could be misinterpreted and fleshed out some of the supporting rationale. It certainly reminded the elders, and the congregation, just how many details go into such an important document and how essential clarity is in its communication. This process was concluded in May 2007.

Churches are not immune to the ebb and flow of social and legal attitudes in the wider world. Some of the external requirements imposed on them change as a direct result of litigation and insurance claim settlements. Cases involving the mistreatment of children were often seen as the most heinous and produced the greatest reactions. Unfortunately, they were beoming more, not less, common. Abuse, whether sexual, emotional or physical, was revealed to be more widespread than previously believed and often systemic within certain environments. Churches and church programs were not immune to this evil, as the wicked practices of some claiming to be loving and caring Christians severely hurt those who should have been safe from predators. Even though Christians should be the first to protect children and other vulnerable individuals, wolves entered and caused tremendous hurt and, in doing so, profaned the name of the Lord Jesus with their actions.

Insurers moved to make institutions, such as churches, much more disciplined in how they operated with vulnerable groups or individuals if they wanted to be covered under specific circumstances. For Trinity to obtain coverage in case a member or worker was found to be guilty of abuse, a series of protocols had to be developed by the church and accepted by the insurer. This included such things as criminal background checks, personal references before being able to volunteer, training on what to do if abuse was suspected, yearly reviews of procedures related to travel, the physical layout of working situations, number of workers present and so on. Much of it seemed invasive and over-the-top, but sin, by its nature is insidious, and it is impossible to know when and where it might emerge. Trinity made all reasonable efforts to develop and put into practice protocols and processes to provide reasonable protection for everyone.

With the help of work done by other churches, the elders produced Trinity's own "Policy to Protect" (originally called the "Abuse Prevention Policy") that initially went into effect in May 2008. Though there were some expectations not entirely applicable to our situation, the requirements of the insurers were met. The goal was to provide an environment that would be safe for both the children and those who looked after them. The church did the practical things needed, but the Lord was looked to as the One who would ultimately keep members, children and visitors safe. Since that time, there have been additional policy statements made connected to other aspects of church life. Some of the details will be mentioned in the next chapter.

Other items of note

There are items of interest that are not sufficiently large to warrant a chapter or even a section within a chapter in a broad history of a church. Nonetheless, it is important to at least note some of them in passing because they have helped shape the worship and service of the people of Trinity and, in some cases, her impact on the wider community. For example, in February 2001, approval was given to install the first *dial-in phone system* for the use of those who were shut-in or simply could not make it out to a given service. It has been used by many people over the years; it helped enable them to feel more a part of the church, even from home. In May 2002, the first discussions were held about moving the evening service time back to 6 p.m.—this was an effort to encourage families with young children to attend, as services would not finish too late in the evening.

Grace Hymns has always been the key source for hymns sung in the services, though the occasional new song would find its way into the bulletin and ultimately into the church repertoire. A few individuals worked hard to collect additional hymns and songs and created two supplementary song books. In December 2004, the church published *Christmas Hymns and Songs*, which greatly expanded the number of selections for singing at Christmas. In October 2005, Trinity produced and began to use its own song book, *Trinity Praise*. This volume of songs included many more recent compositions, as well as more than fifty hymns written by Pastor Payne. A tremendous amount of time and effort was expended behind the scenes to create these volumes and the voluntary and thoughtful spirit put into the work was a great gift to the church as they have been an ongoing blessing to the entire congregation ever since.

The *musicians*[4] at Trinity have always cultivated an atmosphere of praise and worship through their playing. When the organ from the old auditorium was shown to be too small to carry the load in the new building, the church did what any good Baptist church would do: they asked around for one that was in decent shape but no longer wanted and…oh, by the way… free would be great! An excellent organ was, by God's grace, donated to Trinity by a church in the USA and still serves as a support for the worship of God's people.

In June 2005, the *Sunday School* took its first summer off, with classes put on hold until a September restart. This was to give the teachers a bit of a break from weekly preparation and in recognition of the variability of attendance due to family holidays. This became a regular part of the church calendar. With this break the morning service moved up to 10:30 a.m.

To offer some practical assistance to the pastor, the position of *administrative assistant* was proposed to the church. There was broad support for this move and in October 2006, elder Matt Richards was appointed as the first pastoral administrative assistant. As the title suggests, he took on many of the organizational details of the pastor, including some letter

---

[4] See Appendix 2.

writing, document development, visitation, outreach planning, emails and minute-taking. Matt proved to be a valuable support to Pastor Carl.

As an aid to prayer, the missions committee began to produce *monthly prayer calendars* in 2006. And, to help the congregation get to know everyone by name, Trinity's first *photo directory* was published in April 2007.

One of the key channels of communication was the weekly *bulletin*. The first few years of the church bulleting were covered by elder Don Wheaton, then Pastor Payne produced it until his illnesses caused him to pull back. Merry-Lynn Hudson then took it on and produced it faithfully for twenty years. These last few years have been overseen by Andrea Reynolds. This document was, for many years, the key source of printed details regarding the life of the church. The website and church calendar came later, though the bulletin was usually the most up-to-date listing of information. In it one would find details on missions and missionaries (updated information, prayer requests, challenges, blessings, travel plans, administrative and financial needs, projects), prayer requests, preaching and teaching schedules, Scripture texts, quotes, calendar of events (upcoming dates, times and locations), ushers, nursery, conference and special meeting/speaker information, book recommendations, thank you notes and other relevant data. There would be specific prayer requests for other churches, especially the SGF family of churches. There were also notes on anniversaries, births, deaths, engagements, marriages, baptisms, membership, graduations and specific prayer requests for the persecuted church. It is a ministry that required an ear to the ground and a sense of what was happening within the church. The labours of these individuals, and others who stepped in to help, have kept the congregation informed and edified.

The final word goes to the *College & Careers* and *Youth Group* who organized and ran the very first day camp at Trinity. They chose a Saturday in March 2009, and ran *Camp Courageous*! This first outreach effort drew together 44 kids and 22 counsellors. A day of games, stories, challenges, food and biblical lessons was a resounding success and has been repeated most years since then. It was exciting to see the interaction of teens and young adults with the younger kids who, by and large, were thrilled with the attention they got from the "big kids." One of the greatest joys was to see kids from outside Trinity, many of them without a church background, be exposed to the gospel for the first time. May God in His grace and mercy bring fruit from these labours.

6

A decade of testing

The 2010s

◇◇◇◇◇◇◇◇

Thank you

Reading through the minutes of all kinds of meetings that took place over this span of fifty years, it needs to be noted there have been literally thousands of decisions made on an endless stream of issues, such as: allocation of finances, missions support, facility build/rebuild/upkeep, calls to leadership, property management, wasps/ants/bees/ladybugs, water, fire prevention, thermostats, washrooms, painting, instruments, janitorial services, books, benevolence, tapes/CD/videos, Sunday School, the library, special offerings, topics for teaching, plus everything related to all the numerous church ministries. It is impossible to mention all the people who could be thanked for their service. It is encouraging to know the Lord alone noticed each and every one of them and, as He blessed His workers along the way, He will reward them in glory.

Some items of note

In an effort to develop greater consistency among the members when it came to votes on church matters, the board felt it necessary to tighten up the procedure. For a variety of reasons, a significant number of members were failing to cast a vote on serious church matters when given the opportunity to do so. The first step was to clarify the procedures and include supporting explanations as to why they were set up as they were. One of the key elements that needed to be understood was that calculations were based on a percentage of total membership and not simply a percentage of those who cast votes. This meant that any vote not cast resulted in having the same effect as a "No" vote. This was never the intention of members who failed to vote, but it was a consequence, nevertheless. As well, voting could be done by proxy for those who knew they could not make the meeting. A ballot could be filled out in advance and submitted to an elder in a sealed envelope. As a last resort, votes could even be sent in by email to the administrative assistant if there was no concern about him being able to see the vote. As a final check on the completeness of a given vote, a sign-in procedure was instituted the night of the meeting. These steps, and a series of reminders and exhortations to participate, greatly alleviated the problem of the absentee non-vote.

The people at Trinity always had a strong interest in the preparation of young men for the ministry, resulting in many close ties with schools such as TBS. Matt Richards, one of the elders, had sought the Lord's leading in terms of his own potential ministry work. He had preached at Trinity on a few occasions as well as in other churches around southern Ontario. Early in 2010, he began to seriously explore the possibility of pastoral work. He preached several times at two churches who, at the time, were looking for pastoral help. In the end, neither issued him a call at that time. In September, he became aware of the need for a pastor at Jerseyville Baptist Church, a member of the CBOQ.[1] There were some immediate areas of concern, one being the fact that most of the deacon roles were held by women. Matt was encouraged to proceed carefully, as there was a strong liberal element in the CBOQ and some difficult issues might arise as a result. He arranged to meet with the former pastor and then, through

---

[1] The Canadian Baptists of Ontario and Quebec are a group of over 330 Baptist churches.

his opportunities to preach, deal with some particularly foundational doctrines to gauge the response of the congregation. By November, Matt was able to report that the response of the search committee and the congregation to his preaching and his theology were positive and encouraging. As a result, Matt let his name stand for an interim position. An early agenda item would be to encourage men to step up and take on the appropriate roles in leadership, as women had taken on those roles largely because none of the men would. Jerseyville voted that same month to accept Matt as interim pastor for six months, beginning January 1, 2011. He would step down as elder at Trinity for that time period, but he and his wife Andrea would maintain their membership at Trinity until June and await a final vote by Jerseyville. At that point, the people there made their desires clearly known when they voted Matt into the permanent position of pastor, a position he still holds. Trinity sent a letter of congratulations to him and still pray for him as he serves the Lord in that part of His vineyard.

Anyone who has been in a church for any length of time understands things don't always run smoothly within a church family. Issues cover the spectrum from simple to complex, from easily solved to heart-wrenchingly difficult. The elders became aware of one family situation that proved, after prayerful intervention over a period of many months, to be irreconcilable. For the first time, the church was faced with the potential excommunication of a member. It was a difficult time for all involved and the challenge was to be as compassionately biblical as possible. After failing to make real headway through face to face discussions, a letter was sent to the membership indicating that as a next step this individual would have their rights as a member suspended, eliminating the opportunity to serve in any capacity or to vote on church issues. When this did not produce a spirit of confession or repentance, the members gathered for a church vote on excommunication, which passed with a deep sense of sadness but also with a resolve to do what the Lord required in this circumstance. The members sought: (1) to obey Scripture; (2) to honour Christ; (3) to show the seriousness of the sin of disobedience to the clear commands of God; and (4) to see a sinning believer humbled and broken before God and brought to repentance and restoration. It was a humbling time, and much prayer was offered to the Lord that every member of the congregation would remain steadfast in their walk and take nothing for granted when it came to abiding daily in Christ.

In May 2011, the elders had their first meeting with Lois Smith. She was aware that Trinity had been a strong supporter of the Burlington Crisis Pregnancy Centre which had been started by member Jean Laing.[2] Jean gave strong leadership to this work for many years, however, for a variety of reasons, it had eventually ceased operation. Lois had a vision for a similar kind of work in the Hamilton area and was looking for church support before moving forward with the project. The centre would be called Pregnancy Support Services of Hamilton (PSSH).[3] The elders were very much on board and, in January 2012, with the church's approval, financial support for the PSSH began. The centre had its grand opening on March 31, 2012. Since then, Trinity has supported the centre through prayer and financial giving and by participating in their fundraising efforts (Road 2 Hope, Formula 4 Hope and the annual banquet). Praise God for the help they have been to hundreds of women (and men) and the untold number of abortion considerations that became life choosing instead!

As much as everyone enjoyed watching Pastors Payne and Muller try to master the overhead projector at the Christmas Eve service, it was felt a fixed projection and screen system could be beneficial in many situations. Missionaries would often have slide shows or videos to share and it just wasn't possible for them to do it in a way that served the entire congregation. So, in early 2012, with a delicate push from the mission's committee, the deacons got to work exploring audio-visual options. It was a lengthy process as the various needs, restrictions and possibilities offered a variety of paths to follow. In the end, with the proper aspect ratio determined and additional wiring worked out, a system with front screen and rear projector (located behind the screen) was proposed to the church family and accepted. The total cost was about $14,000 and it was installed and used for the first time in October 2013. The system has been of invaluable service in many contexts; the poor old overhead projector is, sadly, no more.

In May 2012, the elders reintroduced a practice once followed by Pastor Payne and began to issue a "Letter from the Elders," doing so about every two months. The goal was to use this communication as a means of keeping the congregation informed of plans and ideas arising from the board, along with justifications and arguments supporting them. It has been used to remind everyone of specific dates and events, items for prayer and praise,

---

[2] See Chapter 3.
[3] In 2019, the name was changed to The Atwell Centre.

areas of concern, updates on changing church policies, details for member meetings and general announcements. There would also be a passage of Scripture with a brief note to encourage the congregation. The elders hoped these communications would be both informative and unifying.

One additional note needs to be made regarding the shift of the start of the Sunday evening service from 6:30 to 6:00 p.m. on a permanent basis. Even though this shortened up the afternoon and created some additional challenges with the youngest and their naps (and perhaps the oldest and their naps), the goal was to make the evening more accessible to parents of slightly older children and not make the time so late that it would have a discouraging effect on getting started on Monday mornings! As in all things, families made the appropriate adjustments and the time soon became the new norm.

The delicate art of hiring (hard choices)

Though the topic of an associate or assistant pastor, or an intern for the summer months, to help Carl with ministry had surfaced in the past, it was not discussed seriously until early 2011. Either scenario would provide an opportunity for a young man, with evident ministerial gifts, to gain some experience with preaching, teaching and operating as part of a board of elders and deacons. The practical benefits both for the candidate and the church could be significant. Being a new program, Trinity had no established structure to use and so other churches and pastors were approached for their recommendations and ideas. This included the leadership at TBS, as well as pastor Stephen Kring at Bethesda Baptist Church in Delhi. Pastor Kring had hired interns before and was instrumental in helping Trinity establish an initial framework of costs, workload and expectations for this new role.

By April, the elders had identified a potential candidate for the part time role of assistant pastor. He first met with Carl for an initial assessment. A document outlining the role and expectations of an assistant pastor was produced and distributed to the board in June for their appraisal and feedback. It included the rationale, responsibilities, remuneration and timeframe of employment. Once approved, it was distributed to the congregation for their consideration. The proposed process would include a trial period of three months, running from October 1 to December 31, at which point a permanent part-time situation might be considered if both parties agreed. Remuneration would be $20,000 per year for two days per week (roughly 16 hours). To help the people and the board with their assessment, the candidate was invited to preach on a few occasions in the summer; his ministry was very well-received.

Through those summer months, procedural details were hammered out. The candidate met with the elders in July for their own round of questions. For the congregation, there would be two steps in voting: (1) vote for the creation of the assistant pastor position itself; and (2) vote for the proposed candidate for the three-month trial period. The candidate would be invited to give his testimony in the evening service of September 11, 2011, followed by a question and answer session with the members on Wednesday, September 14th. At that meeting, a member noted an author referenced by the candidate and pointed out that author did not support a literal rendering and understanding of Genesis 1–2. Where did the candidate stand on this? In his answer, he indicated some uncertainty as to where he absolutely stood at that moment, and that he was still working through various considerations. He affirmed he was still very open to considering a literal understanding as the best position. His response, however, was to be followed up by one of the elders soon after.

The vote to approve the hiring for an interim period was held a week later, on September 21st. Both proposals received enthusiastic approval by the membership. Carl immediately began to arrange a schedule where the new *interim* assistant would begin to lead services and preach the Word.

Over the years, members of the congregation were encouraged to feel free to contact the elders if they had questions or concerns about any area of ministry. One such letter had been submitted back in September 2010, expressing an interest in adding an area of discussion to a Creation seminar that had already been planned and was to be held at the church. Those presenting the seminar were of a young earth worldview, holding that the accounts in Genesis 1–11 should be understood and accepted at face value. The writer of the letter requested that opportunity be given to present an alternative view, one in which the earth could be understood to be very old. A similar request, where alternative viewpoints and perspectives on creation and the age of the earth within the parameters of the adult Sunday School class, had been made earlier. Both requests were declined by the elders on the basis that an old earth position had "insurmountable theological and hermeneutical problems." In a casual discussion with the new assistant pastor, early in the three-month interim period, it became apparent that he was not yet fully persuaded as to which of several positions best articulated his own stance on the early chapters of Genesis.

It was unfortunate this question had not been asked and explored at an earlier stage, something for which the elders took full responsibility (an important lesson learned for future interviews). Since, however, the candidate was still in the formulation stage of determining a position, the elders did what they could to present arguments for and against the various creation models. The candidate was made to understand, from the first weekend after he began, that his decision in this area could certainly be a "make-or-break" one going forward. At points during the interim period, he was encouraged to make a clear determination, if possible, before a vote was held in the new year about moving ahead and the position becoming permanent. The elders attempted to make it clear that anything that swayed from a literal reading of 24-hour days in Genesis 1–2 would be problematic from their perspective; they would not be able to recommend him coming on staff on a permanent basis. At every step, he graciously agreed to consider the matter carefully and prayerfully and be ready to give an account at the appropriate time.

On January 18, 2012, the candidate was given the chance to express, in his own words, his present position on the creation week in Genesis. He did so clearly and honestly; in short, with respect to the best overall view of Genesis 1, he stated he was leaning toward the "framework hypothesis," giving his reasoning in a succinct and understandable manner. After his presentation, he departed and the elders indicated to the members that, based on what had just been expressed, they felt they could no longer support him coming into a preaching/teaching role at Trinity at that time. This meant his name would not be brought forward and there would be no vote for his acceptance. This decision did not sit well with all the members, as this man had showed himself to be an excellent candidate in every other way. The elders were asked to present a summary of their rationale and reasoning for not recommending him and to allow for a discussion on it with the members. A meeting was set for Wednesday, January 25, 2012, for that discussion. The present meeting was adjourned, and people departed in a somber state of mind.

In response to the request by the members, and to help bring some additional clarity to a potentially divisive situation, the elders met to discuss and summarize their position. Once that had been done, the candidate was contacted by the pastor to convey to him the final position of the elders on the issue. As at every other step, the candidate displayed a spirit of grace and understanding. Then, in the next day or so, the elders sent a letter to the congregation outlining the issues as they saw them and the rationale for their actions and decisions. First, some background was offered:

> Discussions regarding our candidate's position on Genesis 1–2 have been ongoing throughout his 3+ months at the church. The elders, after hearing his arguments for the "framework hypothesis" for this passage, remain unanimously convinced that Genesis 1 is an historical passage that must be interpreted in a more literal manner.

A literal approach to the reading of the passage leads to a belief that the earth, and universe, are young, which clearly flies in the face of predominant scientific teaching. The elders also recognized that not all in the church were of a young earth mindset.

> We understand there are some in the church who do not hold to this position and see Genesis 1 in a different light, some along the lines of the candidate's perspective, but some along various other lines. However, we, as elders, do not see compelling reasons within the text itself or in texts elsewhere in Scripture to suggest it means anything other than what it seems to clearly say.

The letter went on to outline several exegetical and theological problems if one allows for an old earth reading into these passages. Arguments by Dr. John MacArthur and Dr. Albert Mohler were also included as support. In the summary, the elders concluded:

> We recognize that there are good men, especially since the early nineteenth century, on both sides of this issue, and we respect and appreciate those who differ with us. While this difference cannot affect our fellowship with Christians of the old earth persuasion, as shepherds of the flock, guarding the deposit entrusted to us, we cannot recommend bringing a man into a preaching/teaching position who holds these views.

With an eye to their own weaknesses and limitations, they closed the letter with,

We have no doubt that, in terms of procedure and communication, this could have been handled with more clarity and leadership. For that we apologize and seek your forgiveness and your ongoing prayers for wisdom as we serve here.

At the meeting on the January 25, the floor was opened to questions from the membership or any comments related to the letter that had been circulated. Perspectives, opinions and arguments on a young versus old earth occupied much of the discussion. Some indicated they felt the candidate had been badly treated by the elders throughout the process. A motion was made to "issue a letter of apology to the candidate for the way he was treated by the board in the application process." It was seconded, discussed and, by a show of hands, was defeated. The process itself had come to a close, but there were some repercussions still to come.

There were many lessons learned through this experience. There was never an intent to cause harm or hurt to the candidate, and certainly no desire to bring unnecessary offense to others in the church. Some members saw this issue as a *secondary* or tertiary one and should not have been allowed to exacerbate the divide between two opposing, but equally acceptable, views. The elders, to a man, were convinced this issue was of *primary* importance and could not be set aside as relatively inconsequential. At an elder's meeting in late January the following is recorded in the minutes:

> The elders agreed unanimously that the theological issue of old vs. young earth was at the core of a fundamental difference in the understanding of the biblical text and exegetical in nature. The elders are committed to a young earth view and a chronological and literal interpretation of the first three chapters of the book of Genesis. The elders also agreed that the church, at this time, was not ready for a divergent view on such an important area of teaching and would not support the "framework" reading of this part of Genesis.

Genesis 1 is the first place in which God reveals Himself, unambiguously, as the Creator of all the universe. Significant aspects of sin, the Fall and the redemption story find their foundations here. Believing Scripture clearly supports the reality of a young earth often results in being "written off" by the wider scientific world as ignorant simpletons for holding to what is undoubtedly biblical myth and legend. The Christian, however, can take great comfort in the veracity, accuracy, trustworthiness and inerrancy of the Word of God, particularly Genesis 1–11. God will ultimately honour those who honour Him. Circumventing, doubting or replacing the clear Word of God will never bring one closer to the truth.

There was some follow-up with members still dissatisfied with the process and the outcome. A couple of letters were submitted with lists of concerns for consideration by the elders. Sadly, when all was said and done, Trinity lost several longtime members and their families in the following weeks and months. Some departed to relocate to more local churches, some because they had lost confidence in the elder's ability or willingness to pursue what they felt was right and proper, some because they felt their opinion didn't really matter and was not heeded and some for reasons totally unrelated to this issue, but it was as good a time as any to make that move. The hurt from all that transpired did not disappear overnight. There was a long period of healing by the Spirit for those who stayed and for those who left, though true resolution was far from universal. God, however, was to be praised and thanked for His kind oversight and grace, especially through those times of challenge and difficulty and, ultimately, all for the good of His church and for His own glory.

Returning to interns

The desire to offer opportunities to train young men was not dampened and, in Fall 2013, work began on a new proposal for a *summer intern* position for the following summer. The church membership agreed that the proposed theological parameters for consideration should include substantial agreement with the *1689 Baptist Confession of Faith*, an amillennial or historic pre-millennial eschatological position, a conservative view on how Sunday should be handled, a belief in the cessation of the miraculous gifts and a young earth perspective on Genesis. With this general structure in mind, a search began with some students from TBS who showed potential in ministerial work. The process got started later than anticipated, but a strong candidate was identified in early April 2014. The elders met with the young man and all indicators seemed positive. The job description with its work expectations was presented at the spring business meeting and an offer of employment for the summer was presented to the candidate. However, at the last minute, he indicated he would not be able to accept the offer for personal reasons. The elders considered doing a quick search for another candidate to serve a shorter term, but decided the Lord was indicating they should wait until the following year.

In early 2015, another candidate was recommended to the elders by the leadership at TBS and, after a couple of very encouraging interviews, Hal Willis was hired as Trinity's first intern. He served the church family well from May through August through his teaching, preaching and fellowship. The experience was so positive that the program continued the next summer bringing Hagop Tchobanian and his wife Ruth to Trinity for the summer months in 2016. Hagop's energetic proclamation of the Word was greatly appreciated by the congregation. The following year another TBS student, Timon Lau, was brought on staff. He and his wife Joanne displayed a strong desire to be of service and were a blessing to the people. The candidate for 2018 was, again, at the last minute, unable to come and minister; the church, at that point meeting at Ebenezer in Burlington, went the summer months without an intern for the second time. In 2019, the church hired one of its own members, Josh Mills, who was in the middle of his MDiv program at TBS. This was an excellent fit for both parties (more to be said on this in the next chapter).

Having an intern serving at Trinity was a wonderful experience for the congregation, as it introduced them to other styles, voices and life experiences. For the candidates, the opportunity to be involved in a leadership position and to learn while working alongside more experienced men, helped them in their own spiritual and character development.

The spectre of litigation

The church's "Policy to Protect" was not the only policy that had to be initiated in a formal manner. Decisions had to be made in other areas as well. Advice received from counsel outside the church encouraged the board to recommend the addition of a number of statements to the church constitution to clarify the church's position on certain issues. The elimination of "vague" or "easily misinterpreted" language was essential as a first step in protecting the church from those who might seek to compel the church to allow practices that were clearly unbiblical. To that end, the following was added to the constitution in "Article 2: Purpose":

> Activities that would fulfill this purpose [the stated purpose of the church in the previous paragraph] would include worship services,

fellowship times associated with those services, prayer meetings, Christian weddings and Christian funerals (as defined by the biblical precepts and teachings adopted by Trinity and applied by the Board) for families in regular attendance at Trinity, Sunday School, Vacation Bible School, mission activities to support missionaries and the agencies through which they serve, fellowship activities and meetings for the entire spectrum of age groups which promote the building up of the church as the body of Christ, and administrative meetings intended to support local Christian Education.

These clarifications would be helpful to the church family in holding their ground if challenged by individuals or groups with inappropriate intentions.

Trinity also decided that the simplest way to deal with the potential for problematic inquiries for renting by those of questionable moral positions would be to close the door to all outside rental inquiries and limit access to those within the church itself. Additional constitutional amendments to the by-laws were made to clarify this stance.

Rental and/or use of the church premises and facilities is limited to families and individuals already considered part of the church congregation, whether members or adherents. Their connection to Trinity has been displayed by consistent, weekly attendance at church services and participation in Trinity functions over a period of time exceeding 12 months.

We will not rent to or allow the facilities to be used by outside agencies or individuals not connected to the church. However, in response to fulfilling our civic responsibility, the facility may be used at times as a voting station for municipal elections if requested by the municipality and our parking lot for occasional training purposes for the local fire department.

Another issue was that of who could/should be married by the pastor or in the church. Again, an addition was made to the constitution under "Article 3: Doctrinal Position," stating the church's stand on the matter.

In light of recent social ethical upheaval, it is essential to note that the church, in accepting Scripture as its statement of faith, believes God created mankind with two genders, male and female (Ge 1:27), that marriage is to be between one man and one woman (Ge 2:24), that sexual relations are intended for a man and woman within a monogamous, married relationship, and that the family unit, consisting of husband and wife and, if God allows, children, is the God-ordained building block of society.

As well, there were government recommendations regarding accessibility and openness to individuals who were dealing with physical or mental challenges. Trinity was already addressing many of these and some did not apply. Increased awareness in the area of special needs is never a bad thing and the church would continue to seek to be aware of situations out of the ordinary and do what was necessary to remove obstacles to worship and fellowship.

A final area was that of transportation. The simple act of picking someone up and taking them to church or a church function was always one of hospitality and service. If, however, the church has "officially" arranged the ride, then a third-party liability policy needed to be in force on behalf of the church. It was getting more difficult for a church family to show kindness to those in need. There was no need, however, to shy away from these displays of Christian love and care; the church just needed to get the litigation bases covered.

Many of these stated positions of the church are not popular with much of the wider world, but they certainly clarified where Trinity stood. In every case, the desire was for a biblical stance. The Lord is to be thanked that, at the time of this writing, Trinity has not been challenged on her position in these areas. Many believe pastors who hold to a strong biblical view on marriage and the family will find their permission to legalize marriages short-lived, since they will not marry couples in a variety of unbiblical situations. However, stands for truth must be taken; the Lord will certainly grant the grace to withstand the opposition and any consequences that arise.

Healing an old wound

In Fall 2015, Carl was contacted by Pastor Aaron Groat of Calvary Baptist Church in Burlington—the same church that had asked Pastor Payne to depart back in 1972.[4] In preparing for the church's anniversary, Pastor Groat had done some exploring of the church's history. When he read church documentation on how they had dealt with Pastor Payne and his family, he was grieved at both the manner of these dealings and the consequences they produced. He contacted Carl to see if he would be able to meet with Pastor Payne and offer an apology on behalf of the church. Carl informed him of his passing almost twenty years prior. He asked if there were still members of the family and if he might be able to contact them. When he learned of Hetty, he was able to speak with her and express his heartfelt sorrow over the events that had transpired more than four decades prior.

He went a step further and invited both Carl and Hetty to the church's anniversary. He also asked if Hetty would bring a word of greeting to the church, which she did with much joy. It was wonderful for her to restore fellowship and meet up with old friends. Certainly, God is the One who keeps records and, in His own way and in His own time, He sets things right, even when it seems to be distant history to His people. Healing may take a long time, but, when it comes, it carries that sweet reality of sins forgiven at the cross of Christ. This is an encouragement to leave things that cannot be solved by human efforts in the hands of the Father.

Odds and bits

One cannot lose sight of the myriad of small things that add together to make the life of a church. Missions continued to be a primary focus of ministry at Trinity as about 40 per cent of the church budget was dedicated to mission work, both home and abroad. Events and programs included men's prayer meetings and breakfasts, a regular ladies Bible study, the College & Careers running Camp Courageous for kids every March, chorale presentations at special events, hosting the SGF Annual General Assembly, support of the PSSH Formula 4 Hope campaign and the shoebox program with Samaritan's Purse every Christmas.

Reading almost any set of minutes, one specific characteristic stood out in the records of the discussion by the elders throughout the years—the phrases "pray for" and "continue to pray for" were repeated over and over at every meeting. People issues can often be complex and must continually

---

[4] See Chapter 1.

be brought to God at the throne of grace. There were prayers for healing, direction, clarification, forgiveness, humility, enlightenment, salvation, revival near and far, new people to join in, restoration of backsliders, the desire and energy to serve, the restraint of Satan and his work and for the Kingdom of God to grow. There was a deep interest in the well-being of sister churches in the SGF and Christ-loving churches beyond. The spiritual life of the people at Trinity was primarily at the heart of the discussions and intercessions of the elders. Far from perfect themselves, they sought to see spiritual growth and increased Christlikeness made more evident in their own lives, as well as in the people under their care. Intercession was a key characteristic of the service the elders sought to offer.

Arson

An early morning call

The day to day demands that rest upon any church congregation are usually sufficient to keep everyone busy. Though there are always things to do, there is an ebb and flow to any given year, marked by slowdowns and recuperation in the summer months, followed by the energetic relaunching of ministries after Labour Day in September. The calendar seemed adequately filled with lots of meetings and services and special events. The Lord, however, sometimes initiates plans for His people that could shake them and rattle them out of what can become comfortable and predictable routines. Always one for encouragement mixed with hard reality, Jesus said, "I have said these things to you, that in me you may have peace. In the world you will have tribulation. But take heart; I have overcome the world" (John 16:33 ESV). Tribulation in the world running hand in hand with peace in Jesus—what a glorious and mysterious paradox! Trials and tribulations come in many forms and, through experience, believers know most of them come through human means. However, simply being familiar with accounts of trials and troubles endured by believers around the world falls short of fulfilling the Lord's instruction of entering into their suffering as if there with them. True empathy can be more elusive if the pathway of experience is exempt from any kind of similar trials. Trinity, while working through a period of relative calm and peace, was about to face an unexpected assault; the Lord, in His wisdom, appointed a night when the congregation's world would be rocked by a severe trial of her own.

Around 1:30 a.m. on Wednesday August 16, 2017, Pastor Muller received a phone call informing him there might be a fire at the church. He dressed quickly and headed for 4372 Appleby Line wondering if this was a prank, a mistake or the real thing. As he neared the church and saw the lights of fire trucks and police cars, followed by a clear view of the flames leaping from the roof of the old church auditorium, he knew it was very real. The fire crews had been called just after 1:15 a.m. and, arriving soon after, battled the blaze with multiple hoses launching thousands of litres of water onto the burning building. Before it was over, more than forty firefighters and twelve trucks were on site attempting to minimize the damage and contain the flames. The fire had been started near the back door where a wooden shed housed one of the oil tanks that fueled the furnace in the old wing. The flames quickly extended up the wall until the wood in the eaves-troughs was ignited. Once the fire reached the roof and attic, it quickly spread from one end of the building to the other. The flames literally lit up the early morning sky! The fire crews were determined to keep the fire restricted to the old building and to save the new addition. With skill, courage and determination—and the evident blessing of the Lord—they succeeded in doing so. The smoldering ruins of the old roof remained the target of huge amounts of water and foam as hot spots were identified and eliminated one by one. The final section of the roof that seemed in imminent danger of collapse was the steeple, badly burned but standing uneasily on four very scorched legs. A final blast of water sent it tumbling into the interior. The battle was over. The fire had done a great deal of damage, but it was stopped before it could travel beyond the old building. A great debt of gratitude is owed to the men and women who fought the blaze on behalf of the church family. Their bravery, professionalism and skill enabled them to harness the destructive power of the fire and minimize its impact on the entire facility. The Lord was merciful in this and should be given thanks for allowing so much of the property to be largely undamaged by anything but smoke and water.

Prior to this event, Trinity was largely unknown to the broader world, but the church became an overnight attraction to TV crews and cameras. Representatives were there from CTV, CHCH, CBC, City TV and others.[5] Photographers from local newspapers took their best shots and the reporters joined the long line of people looking for information. Pastor Muller was

---

[5] See also this interview from *100 Huntley Street*, October 6, 2017; https://youtu.be/Us2Q1Q4ZGro.

Trinity Baptist Church fire on August 16, 2017
Photo © Carl Muller

interviewed on numerous occasions, often on camera. He had prayed that in this time of difficulty and challenge he would be a good witness for the Lord Jesus. Though the news outlets produced the usual spectrum of thoroughness in their reports, ranging from full quotes to disconnected newsbytes, the *Burlington Post* probably ran the most complete representation of events and comments. With respect to the building itself, they quoted Pastor Muller saying,

> We love this building. We'd hate to see it crumble. It means a lot to us because we've been blessed here. It's not that the place itself is sacred, but sacred things have happened here and, so, it breaks our hearts to see it go up in flames.

As a follow up he did remind reporters that "in the deepest sense, the church is not a building after all; the church is the people, and we are still here." When asked about the perpetrators, he suggested,

> I just think it's some malevolent, small-minded people who have done this. I hope they catch them, if in fact it is arson. I would like the chance to talk with them and share the gospel message with them.

In all the feedback received from friends and total strangers via emails, phone calls, personal contact, Facebook and so on, it was apparent the Lord did indeed give him the grace to display a calm spirit and enjoy a clear mind as he represented the Lord and our church family well. Through the many outlets that carried the story, a strong testimony of trust in the goodness and the faithfulness of our Lord was presented to a wide and varied audience. The hope and prayer of the congregation was that the Lord would use this witness as a means of bringing honour to His Name and in the winning of souls to Jesus Christ.

Of course, everyone wanted to know how the fire started. The question of the night was, "Was it accidental or was it arson?" It seemed apparent early on it had been deliberately set, based on the location of the initial blaze outside the buildings. If this had been all, the buzz would probably have died down in 48 hours, as Trinity's story would be quickly replaced by new news from around the world. However, the presence of some bold and pointed graffiti on the church walls had reporters asking about religious intolerance and hate crimes—headings which catch a lot more

Trinity Baptist Church on the morning of August 16, 2017
Photo © Mark Hudson

attention than "Country Church Set on Fire by Local Arsonist." The painted comments don't need to be given additional print here. If the intent of the arsonists was to stir up anger and a judgemental spirit of resentment or revenge, the church congregation gave clear evidence of the exact opposite. The hand of a sovereign God, who loved them as His own children, was overseeing even this difficult event for their good. As a result, prayers of thanksgiving were offered for the saving of the main part of the church structure and that no-one had been injured. Prayer was also offered for those responsible, that they would, in time, be convicted in their hearts and consciences by the Spirit of God and be converted to the Lord Jesus.

An oft-heard phrase on the lips of the people was "The true church is not a building, it's the people of God" and this was both true and comforting. There was still, however, a great feeling of loss and sadness for many in the congregation, especially those who had spent much of their Christian life worshipping in that building. Those old brick walls had witnessed weddings, baptisms, worship services, prayer meetings and other memorable events over the years and made that century-plus structure incredibly special. This would certainly be true as well for those church families that pre-dated Trinity. Zimmerman church had stood since 1890 and several generations of members and adherents would have pleasant memories of events held there. Some contacted the church with notes of sympathy and encouragement. Charter members of Trinity, some of whom were still at the church, could recall the financial sacrifices made to purchase and restore the church for congregational use back in 1975–1976. They knew the Lord had been with them in discovering the church for sale, in allowing the congregation's offer of purchase to be accepted, the retirement of the initial mortgage shortly thereafter and all the additions and alterations made to the facility since. They, along with those who had begun attending Trinity since its inception, had no doubt the Lord would be faithful to them still as they moved forward from this major physical and emotional setback.

The outside response from other Christians started arriving virtually the moment the fire had been extinguished. Emails and phone calls kept Pastor Muller busy, even as he stood on the roadside watching the final efforts of the fire department to douse the remaining hot spots. Some of the elders were in contact with one another and felt it prudent to cancel the upcoming Sunday morning service; another location for the church to gather would have to be determined. The Lord, who was still overseeing all

A decade of testing 133

After the fire, showing the damage to the library and the old sanctuary
Photo © Mark Hudson

things for good, was in the process of providing the church with a very gracious and timely offer. One of the first people to contact the pastor by phone was an individual from Crossroads Centre in Burlington, offering, at no charge, the use of their chapel for morning and evening services as long as it was needed—and it was available for use that very Sunday morning! Praise God for His impeccable timing and for the kindness and thoughtfulness of His loving and compassionate people. So, before the leadership could even begin to compile a list of possible alternate locations, it was settled!

Throughout that first morning, many other offers of help flowed in from individuals, churches and community groups. Some offered the use of their facilities for prayer meetings, Bible studies and other ministries, and, if it would be helpful, others were ready to take in at least some of Trinity's people until they could get resettled. People were asking if there was a way to contribute to the rebuild in terms of money and/or labour. The people of God, when they became aware of this situation, mobilized around the throne of grace and interceded powerfully and compassionately on behalf of the Trinity Baptist Church family. They prayed for courage, confidence and wisdom and, from the outset, the Lord answered those prayers with an outpouring of sustaining grace, a tangible sense of peace and the provision of an unflagging trust in the good Shepherd.

The immediate aftermath

In the case of a fire of this nature, the police and fire departments take charge of the scene to ensure public safety. As well, with arson suspected, the site became a crime scene and, for most of the rest of that day, the police and the Office of the Fire Marshall (OFM) were present conducting their investigations. Detectives were busy collecting information and evidence that might lead to the arrest of the arsonist(s), while the fire marshall worked to determine what means was used to start the fire. Late that Wednesday afternoon, after completing their research, they signed the building back over to the church. Their final report would come out later with their analysis and conclusions. The insurance adjuster had been on site since early in the morning and had groups standing by to start dealing with the aftermath. An emergency response team would be on site the next morning to start cleaning up and securing the site. Overnight security was assigned to the property to ensure no additional vandalism took place and to prevent interested bystanders from getting into areas of potential danger.

The church was well represented that day, specifically through the specialized work of three of our deacons: Nathan Droogendyk (a civil engineer), Justin Dokter (construction) and Scott Spencer (church treasurer). These men were used by God to help interpret what was being said, done and proposed by the engineers on site. Though many people stepped in to help, these three men in particular would commit many additional personal hours to the follow-up work over the next several months.

At the recommendation of the adjuster, the company ServiceMaster was employed by the church to immediately deal with several important tasks:

1. Identify and deal with all church contents based on their condition and help the adjuster to separate between recoverable and non-recoverable items.
2. Clean and store all recoverable items until they could be returned to the church
3. Clean out all damaged drywall, ceiling tiles, floor tiles, shelves, cupboards, loose items, etc.
4. Help arrange for restored power to the site
5. Dry the facility out to prevent mold.

They had a crew of about a dozen people start on this work the Thursday morning after the fire. A security fence was put up around the property, broken windows boarded up and access restricted to workers and representatives from the church.

Damage by fire, smoke and water

The original church structure

The fire was started at the southwest corner of the old building. Flames climbed a short section of wall, ignited the eaves above and crossed into the attic space and roof above the old auditorium. By the time the fire was extinguished, most of the roof was burned away or collapsed with some additional fire damage to the adjoining roof of the adjacent extension. The old rafters were still in place, though badly charred. The interior was largely untouched by flames but severely damaged by falling debris, water and smoke, including the library, much of which was, amazingly enough, left standing and visually intact. The lower two thirds of the stained glass window dedicated by the Bennett family was melted away, though the remaining upper third could possibly be recoverable. A quick glance into the basement area showed walls and ceilings soaked and damaged beyond repair. At the very least, there would have to be a gutting of the entire interior and a complete rebuild, assuming the outer structure itself was redeemable.

The additions and new wing
Other than fire damage to a section of roof in the senior nursery, damage to all the additions was limited to smoke and water. The main auditorium was the least affected and, after a good cleaning, could be back in operation quickly. (Though eventually it was determined the carpet had to be replaced.) The Fellowship Hall had at least 4 inches of water at the height of the flood and required the bottom two feet of drywall to be removed all the way around, as well as all the floor tiles. The fire retardant covering the main supporting I-beams in the ceiling would have to be removed and reapplied. The bathrooms were stripped to the studs and all sinks and toilet fixtures removed. Most of the shelves and cupboards in the kitchen absorbed water and would have to be replaced. The elevator shaft had to be drained of water and many new cables and connectors installed. Beyond the top of the ramp, in the hall leading to the Sunday School classrooms, most walls were taken down to their studs and all ceiling tiles and supports removed. Upstairs, in the nursery area, all the carpets were ripped out and most of the drywall removed. The good news was, most of this damage could be reversed with fresh materials, some replacement parts and a fresh coat of paint. The main underlying structure of the 2004 addition suffered little damage from the fire and water.

Untouched, recoverable, non-recoverable
There were three categories into which the contents of the various rooms and closets fell. The first included anything not affected by water, fire or smoke; the adjuster determined early on that nothing in the church fell into that category. The second category included all items considered recoverable; they would be removed from the premises, cleaned and stored until after restoration. Category three included any item classified "beyond clean/restore" and thus deemed non-recoverable; these items would eventually be replaced by a new equivalent or something of similar value. ServiceMaster undertook this massive project and, with the help of the adjuster and members of Trinity, designated every object, book, toy, desk,

chair, shelf, etc. into one category or the other. All items to be replaced (such as the entire library) would be assigned a monetary value which would be used to purchase replacement items. There was going to be a long shopping list in the not-too-distant future.

A complicating factor

On Thursday morning, the day after the fire, a structural engineer was on site, mainly to examine the state of the walls and roof of the burned building and begin to determine its structural integrity. He was also tasked with making recommendations on what next steps would be prudent in terms of safety and, eventually, reconstruction. As he examined the area near the origin of the fire, he noted the presence of a fuel oil smell. Looking more closely, the fuel oil was seen to be on the ground around and near the fuel tank that supplied the furnace in the old sanctuary. From the burn marks on the storage tank, it appeared it may have been nearly full while the fire burned, but now it was almost empty. If this proved to be true it meant a possible 800–850 litres of diesel fuel oil had leaked from the tank and onto the ground. This had the potential to become an even greater concern than the fire and water damage of the previous day. Mercifully, it was determined the spill was caused by the fire (the weakening of a gasket around the fuel filter) and, therefore, the church's insurance coverage automatically kicked in.

The lead engineer, with some experience with this kind of spill, began the process—one that became a very long process—of tracking the oil. Where did it all go? An initial investigation tracked oil through underground drainpipes across the back of the church, with some amounts emptying into the ditch along No. 2 SR, leading down to Bronte Creek. Traces of oil were found in the ditch itself and so, to prevent additional oil getting though, the engineers blocked the flow from the pipe on church property with a temporary catchment basin.

With a contaminant spill, certain protocols immediately go into effect. For anything on the premises, the Technical Standards and Safety Authority (TSSA) is called in and, for anything that leaves the premises into the surrounding land, the Ministry of the Environment (MOE) is notified. The initial purpose of both groups is to assess the extent of the spill, attempt to contain it and then give direction as to how the spill is to be cleaned up. Representatives of both groups arrived and began their own investigations.

The MOE determined, relatively quickly, that, even though some oil had left the property, the damage that would be done to dig it out, all the way down to the creek, would be much greater than any damage caused by the oil itself. Therefore, no action would be taken to remediate that area. The fuel oil on the property itself was another story!

After some exploratory drilling and digging around the foundation, oil was located at the north end of the building. This was a surprise. Determining how it got there would be the primary challenge for many months. It was a long and frustrating process, trying to track the mysterious path the fuel had taken. It had not circumnavigated the entire church structure, as there were sections along three sides with no discernible traces of oil. Engineers were convinced it had travelled *under* the buildings from the south to the north and then circled back to the east and west sides through the weepers along the base of the foundation. Sadly, the path(s) remained stubbornly hidden. Until these could be identified and delineated, plans for cleanup were on hold.

To eliminate the possibility of further responsibility for potential cleanup in the future, the insurance company was determined that all contaminated soil should be removed. This also fell in line with the expectations of the NEC; the church building sat on NEC land classified as "sensitive," therefore requiring the concentration of oil in the ground to be reduced to 0 ppm. This left little wiggle room for the engineers.

The church family was brought up to speed on the initial steps in the cleanup process at a meeting after the morning service on August 27th. The services were then being held at Crossroads Centre in Burlington. A motion was made and accepted to provide the board with the greatest possible leeway in the utilization of funds made available from the insurers based on policy limitations and guidelines. It was also agreed a law firm be engaged to offer oversight in any legal matters that might arise.

There had been several additions/alterations to the original 1890 church building: in 1976, 1986, 1996 and 2004. As a result, there were lots of underground conduits inserted, altered, removed, connected, plugged or left. Which underground pathway the oil had taken was still unknown. Complicating the situation was the lack of access to the basement of the old church building itself due to safety concerns. If the internal guts of the old building were to be removed (charred roof trusses, fallen debris from the roof, the main floor and its contents, the walls and contents of the basement) to be able to access the concrete basement floor to "drill

Demolishing the 1890 Zimmerman section of the church
Photo © Joel Reynolds

for oil," the walls would need to be structurally stable. Even with some creative and extensive (and costly!) bracing initiatives, this did not offer a promising outcome and, after long discussion, was not seen as a viable or safe route to go. The only other practical alternative was to raze the 1890 building to the ground. This recommendation was a very painful one for the board to make as the 1890 building was a recognized symbol of the gospel's history in the area and a significant witness to Trinity's part in that history. It had been the distinguishing feature of the church facility for anyone travelling up Appleby Line from the south for over a century. It was with great sadness the board knew it had to be removed to get on with the rest of the cleanup and eventual rebuild. Even though several officials at the city level indicated they wanted to allow the church to move ahead with this, the process of applying for and receiving demolition permits was painfully slow. The nice weather of the fall quickly disappeared, and the demolition did not begin until November 15, 2017! The demolition only took a few days; the gaping hole that remained seemed a poor memorial to the honourable structure that once stood on that spot.

With the removal of the 1890 building, the exposed ground allowed for the identification of the mysterious pipe-to-pipe connections that had carried oil from the south end over to the east, then north, then west walls of the addition. The satisfaction of discovery was brief, however, as the extent of the oil seepage still had to be identified and then all the damage it had caused fixed.

After many test holes were dug to check for the depth and extent of the underground oil plume, and most of the walls around three sides of the 2004 building had been excavated to the foundation, final recommendations were made regarding how best to manage and engineer the cleanup. Anywhere the church sat on virgin soil, contaminants had travelled a very short distance. There were several places, however, where the foundation sat on compacted stone which made the potential for oil travel much greater. While trying to track its movement, several portions of the inside basement floor were dug up and removed; the soil under the building was then tested. Early on there was concern that large portions of the basement floor alongside the exterior walls might have to be removed if oil had migrated through the stones under the foundation and reached a position under the floor itself. A process of remediation was adopted involving underpinning. Wherever there was evidence of oil migration near the outer walls, the stones beneath the foundation were removed in sections and the foundation underpinned with fresh concrete. Some sections required a different technique, utilizing concrete piles inserted in the ground outside the foundation line and then bolted with steel plates to the foundation. This was a long and costly part of the work but, after several weeks, it was completed. Most of the three walls of the new addition had been underpinned in one way or another. At this point, all the contaminated soil had been removed, the foundation secured and the basement walls backfilled. The church building now seemed ready to withstand an earthquake up to a 7.0 on the Richter Scale!

The majority of oil had, fortunately, descended down into the soil near the rear entrance, where the oil tank had been situated. It reached a depth of about 14 feet and spread horizontally under the southwest end of the 1890 structure, as well as under the south section of the senior nursery. To get access to some of this soil was another reason it became necessary for the old building to come down. Losing part of the nursery was unfortunate, but unavoidable.

Historical revelation

One of the unexpected surprises during the demolition was the discovery of four time capsules from 1890 in the form of cylindrical tin containers with lids. One had been placed in each of the four corners of the old foundation. One of these had opened during demolition and its contents were found blowing around the construction site; fortunately, the contents were retrieved. The most intriguing item from that first opened capsule was a poster advertising the laying of the cornerstone of Zimmerman Methodist Church on Tuesday, July 29, 1890, at 3:00 p.m. The key individuals involved were Mrs. Wm. Kerns, Mrs. Johnson Zimmerman, Mr. Massey (of Massey & Co., Toronto) and Jno. Foster, Esq., Lowville. Tea was to be served at 5:00 p.m. (at a cost of 25 cents) after which addresses were to be delivered by Revs. Jno. Wakefield, Geo. Clark, Geo. Ferguson and others. Music would be provided by the Waterdown Methodist choir. In fine print at the bottom of the add it was noted, "Any offerings laid on the stone will be thankfully received by the Trustee Board." It was good never to miss giving people an opportunity to donate to the work.

It would have been an exciting time for that church family to see this simple but very respectable building open for worship. Some of the other preserved documents gave insight as to the nature of the immediate cultural and historical context in which they sought to serve the Lord. Methodists were numerous in the Niagara region, which included the various districts and their associated circuits spread through Welland, Niagara Falls, Woodstock, Simcoe, Milton, Waterdown, Hamilton and several other small towns in between. Copies of the 1887, 1888 and 1889 *Minutes of the Proceedings of the Niagara Annual Conference of the Methodist Church* were found in the cannisters. The sixth session, in 1889, was held at King St. Church in the town of Ingersoll, June 5th to 12th. Some of the items of business that would have been of interest to Zimmerman's first congregation would include the election of the president and various secretaries, a listing of where each minister would be serving in the upcoming year, numbers of members / baptisms / marriages in that year by circuit (about 26,000 members, just under 900 marriages), how much money was collected by circuit (about $250,000 collected in all areas of ministry) and a name by name list of everyone who had contributed $5 or more to the minister's fund. There were pages and pages of statistics of this sort. There was a long series of reports by the various committees that seemed to oversee every aspect of the Methodist world. For example, the Temperance Committee reported in their Item 7, "That we strongly condemn the present political parties for their truckling silence in their campaign documents and public addresses on the question of immediate prohibition of the liquor traffic."[6] They encountered the deafened ears of government officials in their own day; one can only imagine their wonder at the battles Christians face today.

From the Committee on the State of the Work they offered, as Item 1,

> That, believing it to be the Divine plan to convert the world through the preaching of the Gospel applied to the consciences of men by the power of the Holy Ghost, we cannot too strongly emphasize the apostolic direction, "Preach the Word." Preach repentance to the sinner, faith to the penitent, and holiness to the believer. As ambassadors of the Lord Jesus Christ we should ever feel the responsibility of our position, and hence, whatever aid we might secure in the prosecution of our work, we should never forget that we are responsible for the doctrines presented and for the instruction given.[7]

---

[6] *Minutes of the Proceedings of the Niagara Annual Conference of the Methodist Church* (1889), 48.
[7] *Minutes of the Proceedings of the Niagara Annual Conference of the Methodist Church* (1889), 49.

CORNER STONE

The Corner Stone of the New

ZIMMERMAN

METHODIST CHURCH

will D. V., be laid on

TUES., JULY 29,

at 3 p. m. by the following parties:

Mrs. Wm. Kerns, Mrs. Johnson Zimmerman, Mr. Massey (of Massey & Co., Toronto), and Jno. Foster, Esq., Lowville.

At 5 p.m. Tea will be served by the ladies, after which addresses will be delivered by Revs. Jno. Wakefield, Geo Clark, Geo. Ferguson and others. Music by the Waterdown Methodist Choir.

ADMISSION TO TEA, - 25 CENTS,

And any offerings laid on the stone will be thankfully received by the Trustee Board.

July 23rd, 1890. [Reformer Print.]

A poster about the setting of the corner stone of Zimmerman Methodist Church on Tuesday, July 29, 1890, discovered in one of the time capsules

There were a number of handwritten lists (a reminder of the day when beautiful, flowing cursive writing was the norm) perhaps showing membership by name at local churches. One was marked "Lowville" and included the names of the official board of the Lowville and Zimmerman circuit, identifying trustees, superintendents and so on. In one envelope, marked Maggie Wilson, there was a list of about 80 people (11 of whom were Zimmermans) with dollar amounts ranging from $0.25 to $50; perhaps these were amounts given toward the cost of the new building.

To help those in the present to understand the world of 1890, several publications were included that could give a broad sense of what was going on locally and around the world. Along with a copy of *The Christian Guardian* (a weekly publication of the Methodist church) were recent copies of *The Globe* (Toronto), *The Canadian Champion* (Milton), *The Empire* and the *Hamilton Spectator*. One interesting comment in the *Globe* from Tuesday, July 29, 1890, was an editorial response from one Malcolm Gibbs. He notes, "I was much pleased with your article in favour of abolishing personal taxation, and I hope you will keep up the agitation until this evil is removed from our midst. The present system puts a premium on untruthfulness, and the dishonest man escapes his full payment of taxes while the honest citizens pay more than their share. Give us a business tax."[8] And by the way, if anyone is looking for Wm. Beith and wife, from Whitby, they are staying at the Queens (personal section of the *Globe*).

In quite good condition was a copy of *Massey's Illustrated*, Vol. 2, No. 7, July 1890. Members of the Massey family were probably central figures in the work at Zimmerman. Along with ads for all things related to the farm (combination mower knives, composite silver binder twine, Wilson's Hay Tools of Hamilton and Myers' Spice for your horses and cattle), were several articles targetting the broader agricultural community. There were crop reports from across Canada and from around the world, as far away as Australia. The twelfth and final chapter, of what might have been an around-the-world travel log, was recorded from the pen of W.E.H. Massey and covered, in some detail, his explorations and observations. He reported from the Mediterranean, many sites in Italy, then observed icebergs off Newfoundland and vibrantly expressed his wonder and awe at the Forth Bridge in Scotland ("one of the greatest scientific and mechanical

---

[8] *The Globe* (Tuesday, July 29, 1890), 4.

The Zimmerman Methodist Church congregation in 1891
Source: Burlington Historical Society

achievements of modern times"[9]). Not to ignore the needs and interests of the ladies of the period, an essay entitled, "Good Housekeeping" by Mrs. G.A. Forbes of Waterdown, Ontario, was included and took up an entire page of fine print. It is no wonder it was awarded second prize in a Massey essay writing contest. She got right to the point and, in the opening paragraph, affirmed,

> In order to have a well-kept house, there are two essential qualifications required, namely: system and order. The lady who, either in the oversight or actual performance of the everyday duties devolving upon her, has a systematic and orderly method, will accomplish more, and of a better quality, than another whose work is done in a haphazard, go-as-you-please manner.[10]

---

[9] *Massey's Illustrated*, Vol. 2, No. 7 (July 1890): 3.
[10] *Massey's Illustrated*, Vol. 2, No. 7 (July 1890): 4.

She went on to explain that by doing a roast, with potatoes and beans, with an apple pie, on Monday, the top of the stove would be free to do the laundry without encumbrance. Fortunately, she just as clearly laid out all the duties for the other days of the week, along with supporting rationale for all things domestic. Her logic and practicality were, no doubt, well received and practiced extensively in the community. It would be interesting to see what essay was awarded first place.

Some items in the containers would have to be examined by a person who specialized in older, worn documents. The church would make decisions on what should be preserved and put on display in the church, what should be put into safe storage and what might be of interest to local historians.

As a follow-up, Trinity created their own time capsule and included some of the material from the original ones. To this the church added their own significant documents and sealed them behind the recovered 1890 cornerstone in a special location in the rebuilt 1890 (now 2020) structure. There is a plan for a permanent display of some of the time capsule contents for everyone to see and enjoy. Perhaps the Lord will allow another 127 years before this time capsule is examined!

Costs

Trinity Baptist Church, of course, had insurance coverage. They had, however, switched over to a new provider about fifteen months prior to the fire. Their adjuster was on site the very first day and worked hard to help the board understand the various limits and provisions of the policy. At that initial stage, there were four possible areas of financial responsibility for the church:

1. A co-insurance clause in the policy held the church responsible for a percentage of the costs if the overall coverage was less than 90 per cent of the estimated replacement value of the entire property. The first draft of this estimate, made by a third-party evaluation, indicated the church might have to foot the bill for at least 10 per cent of the costs of repair. On an extreme repair bill of $3 million this would come to about $300,000. From the outset the board felt the initial estimate of the property value was too high and so documentation was collected and presented to the adjuster challenging some of the details and assumptions of the assessment. The goal

was, in a fair and reasoned way, to reduce the church's financial responsibility to zero, if possible. This would take a number of months of consideration on behalf of the insurer but, in the end, this co-insurance amount was reduced to zero. The Lord had once again shown His hand of mercy on the church family.
2. If the total cost of repair and restoration were to exceed the policy limits, the church would be responsible for 100 per cent of the additional costs. The church was blessed by the fact that there were additional insured amounts beyond the basic policy that helped absorb specific expenses, such as costs related to engineer and professional fees and an amount for oil remediation.
3. If the decision was made to upgrade any replacements allowed by the insurer, the church would have to absorb the additional costs. For example, the plan was to switch from oil heating to propane; if the insurer allowed a certain amount to replace the oil furnaces and propane furnaces cost more, the church would absorb the difference.
4. Insurance would not cover the portion of HST[11] the church could recover. This resulted in a temporary outlay of money, as the church would have to pay its portion of the HST as bills came in. Every six months, however, the treasurer would submit a request to reclaim this portion of the HST, so the church would recover this money down the line. It required a short-term cash flow, possibly in the total amount of about $100,000. The insurance company assisted in this area by forwarding the church a portion of the cash value they would eventually award to replace the 1890 building, thus helping tremendously with cash flow.

Not knowing it at the time, but eventually being out of the church building for over two years created a drastic change in some previously predictable income/expense items. Amounts for things such as heating, hydro, building maintenance, projects and improvements, Sunday School, library and many others became unpredictable. No significant alterations were made to the church budgets over that period of time as dollar amounts would have to be based on best guesses and anticipated costs. More stable items such as salary, mission support and ministry work remained in

---

[11] Harmonized Sales Tax.

operation. The board was thankful for the constancy of God's people in terms of their prayer support, attendance and regular financial giving enabling these commitments to be met, unabated by the challenges flowing from temporary relocation.

Looking back at a church home from 1890–2017

The Zimmerman Methodist Church building was opened on July 29, 1890. With some of that history detailed elsewhere (see *Trinity Baptist Church: Beginnings*, published 1997), it is not essential to lay it out again here. However, with the completion of the demolition of the old structure, it is important to pause and reflect on how much church life it housed over its 127 years. It has passed through three main bodies of believers. The Methodists built the church and utilized it from 1890 to 1925, then, after the church union, it became, along with Lowville, the Lowville-Zimmerman United Church with a shared pastor. They ceased their regular meetings there in 1970 and the property was then purchased by Trinity Baptist Church in 1975 with the congregation moving in, after renovations and a small addition, in 1976. There are many people still in the Trinity congregation who enjoyed years of services spent in the old auditorium. For some it was the first place they heard preaching on the great doctrines of grace; for others it was where they were baptized or married. People who joined the church after the new wing was completed in 2004, remember the auditorium of the old wing more as a classroom and a library. From the outside, it became the iconic image of the church, strikingly visible as you approached from the south on Appleby Line. To see the building partially burned, and then to see it gone altogether, has caused more than a few tears among the people and those in the immediate neighbourhood. Even though the congregation understands it was just a building, their hearts told them it was their special church home.

Perhaps the most memorable characteristic of that space was the echo of faithful men preaching the Word of God. Pastor Payne was at the heart of that preaching from the day it reopened in 1976 to his death in 1997. Pastor Muller carried that same spirit forward since that point; the sanctuary was regularly filled with excellent expository preaching and teaching.

It seems the original architects knew what was required in a building to promote great singing. Whether with the piano and organ together or one instrument at a time, the people were exhorted to sing with a spirit that gave a felt substance to the worship of God. That old sanctuary had been special to so many people!

Restoration and rebuild

No one imagined how long it would take to turn from cleanup and tear down to restore and rebuild. It was not until the first week of September 2018, that the cleanup work resulting from the spilled oil was finally completed, more than twelve months after the fire. This involved the removal of all contaminated soil, the demolition of the 1890 structure and the filling and compacting of the land immediately south of the old building to allow for future construction and parking. At this point, the internal work could finally be tackled.

The board had recommended to the church family that the restoration be broken into three major phases.

Phase 1: Oil remediation

The removal of contaminated soil and alterations to the 2004 foundations have already been detailed. There were many areas of frustration throughout this process. One in particular arose as a result of lack of consistency in communications with outside groups. Too often procedures and rationale were not clearly defined and, even when they were, they were not always closely followed. To help with this, Trinity needed their "own man" on the jobsite to act as a bridge between the church and the external companies. Early in this process, then, the membership approved the hiring of an external engineering specialist to advocate for the church and her interests. His recommendations and insights on many aspects of this remediation work were very valuable and helped keep the work moving forward at a steady pace.

Phase 2: Restoration of the 2004 addition

There were unexpectedly long delays in obtaining details on the scope of repairs to be done to restore the 2004 extension. Once this was finally available, the plans for restoration proceeded. As in all cases of dealing with the municipality, there were permits to be applied for and waited upon. This involved the submission of a complete set of drawings, including all the necessary mechanical, electrical and structural details. This, of course, required time and money! Once the permits were granted, several companies were offered the opportunity to bid on the work. With only two companies submitting bids in the time allowed, the work was granted to Kamphuis Construction and Restoration from Vineland. Their work began the middle of September with an initial projected finish date of mid-January 2019. The board recommended taking this opportunity to make beneficial alterations to parts of the various extensions. Since the insurers would only cover costs to "put it back the way it was," any additional costs related to these alterations would have to be covered by the church. In preparation for this contingency, the board requested, and was granted by the membership, permission to spend up to an additional $100,000 on these upgrades. These included changing from oil to propane furnaces, an expansion and redesign of the sound booth area in the main auditorium, the reconfiguring of the south set of stairs to the balcony, shifting a few walls, a new kitchen in the "new old" building and additional washroom space off the narthex.

Phase 3: Replacement of the 1890 building and connecting classrooms
During the final stages of Phase 1 and, while discussions were being held regarding the upgrades to the 2004 addition, an eye was cast toward the eventual construction of the new building on the 1890 site. In consultation with several church committees (representing the major church ministries), general plans were made to tie together the upgrades of the old with the design of the new. This was necessary to avoid redoing parts of Phase 2 to make Phase 3 work. It was a fluid process that juggled various needs and interests; discussions produced widely acceptable results in the shaping and reshaping of the floor plans allowing the maximum benefit to the widest number of ministries.

Relocation

The Lord looked after the church family in every area while away from home. It has been noted that the first open door was at Crossroads Centre in Burlington on the Sunday morning immediately after the fire. In their facility they had a lovely chapel that sat about 200 people. It came equipped with pews, piano, hymnbooks, a room for a nursery and a usable sound system. Perhaps the only negative was a lectern/pulpit made of plexiglass that shuddered and shook at the lightest touch; it was delicate but proved to

A decade of testing 151

be sufficient for the task, never collapsing when it seemed it would. Other than having to vacate for previously booked events on a couple of occasions, worship proceeded in a comfortable manner for several months. Some new families and individuals even joined in during that time.

The next big move was initiated by the sale of the Crossroads facility to a private individual. The new owner allowed the continued use of the chapel until the end of March 2018, at which point planned renovations made it impossible to stay. With only four weeks to find a new location, several alternatives were quickly explored. It was a challenge to find a spot with a large enough venue available at or near the usual worship times. One of the elders reminded the board of a church in Burlington who had offered help soon after the fire. Upon checking with a couple of members of their board, discussions were held, and permission granted to use Ebenezer Canadian Reformed Church on Dynes Road in Burlington. It was more than a little ironic that Ebenezer had been through their own fire a number of years back, when their entire old structure burned to the ground. This led to the eventual construction of the present building on Dynes Road.

With their services at 9:30 a.m. and 3 p.m., Trinity opted to hold services at 11:30 a.m. and 6:30 p.m. It was a later start time than usual, but the people soon adjusted, and the times became routine. The quiet and relaxed start to a later morning service was probably missed by some when the 9:45 a.m. Sunday School bell began to ring again back in the new building.

Due to a lack of space, Sunday School was not offered at either Crossroads or Ebenezer. This ministry was greatly missed; the plan was to start again soon after getting back to Appleby Line. Kids Club had also been largely put on hold, though occasional meetings and outings were held with plans for additional meetings in Fall 2018. The ladies Bible study met at Calvary Baptist Church from September 2017 to May 2018. This was also the sight of a baptismal service for some new members. St. George's Anglican Church was of inestimable help by allowing the use of a room for prayer and board meetings, as well as the main hall for special meetings and dinners. Starting in September 2018, they also hosted the ladies Bible study. A big plus from this relationship manifested itself when several of the ladies from St. George's joined in with the Trinity ladies for the studies! What an excellent opportunity for fellowship and helping others grow! Even after moving back to Appleby Line, this group continued to meet at St. George's for study.

The people of Trinity were greatly moved by the generosity and kindness of their brothers and sisters in Christ at these various locations. Their willingness to help in time of need made them channels of blessing and gracious gifts from our heavenly Father. Trinity would like to be as willing and quick to help others in like manner, if given the opportunity in the years to come. The Lord will indeed bless these friends for all for their attentiveness and care and the sacrifices they made on behalf of believers in need.

The road back home

Kamphuis Construction originally suggested they would need 120 days to complete the work in the scope of repair. The actual physical work of Phase 2 got underway the first week in October 2018, with an initial completion date set for early February 2019. After a few weeks, however, that date was found to be extremely optimistic. Phases 2 and 3 overlapped in such significant ways that some elements of the Phase 2 work had to be delayed and then altered to avoid reconstructing when Phase 3 work began. With the desired alterations and improvements incorporated, the board proposed plans to the membership for the Phase 3 rebuild and the resulting domino effects on the remainder of the work on Phase 2. This took place at a meeting on March 6, 2019. The additional costs to Trinity, over and above insurance reimbursement, could now range between $150,000 and $390,000. The general response from the membership was very positive and they approved the proposed plans with the additional spending at a membership meeting on March 17. The final work on Phase 2 could now proceed with a new finishing date of August 2019. While this was taking place, architectural drawings were produced for the new building and application made for permits to build.

It would be wonderful to report there were no additional obstacles and challenges tossed into the mix. However, just as a pastor might give some slight, hopeful indication that he is drawing his already longish sermon to a close, only to surprise his congregation with several bonus points that just came to mind, the end of this process shifted back to a more distant horizon. Some required reports from some quarters outside the church took an exceptionally long time to be completed and submitted to the city. The slow pace with some city officials was also frustrating at times, though there were assurances Trinity was being given high priority; those groups who treated Trinity's situation as such were greatly appreciated.

A potentially fatal blow to the rebuild was delivered via a communication from the Halton Region in late spring. It stated that even though assurance had been given all along that a rebuild on the same footprint would be allowed without having to apply for variances and setbacks, there might now be a complication. Someone had raised the spectre of a weakened hillside leading to Bronte Creek due to two factors: (1) the large hole that had been dug to remove the oil at the south end of the property and (2) the underpinning process applied to the west wall of the 2004 structure. After submitting supporting geotechnical evidence to the contrary, the Region eventually rescinded their concern. There were great sighs of relief around the board; once again the Lord had intervened for His people.

Throughout the summer months, work on Phase 2 continued in stop and start fashion; waiting for permits and the availability of trades at the necessary times once again extended the timeline for completion. However, rumours of a possible early fall finish date began to circulate in midsummer and, in the Lord's mercy, it appeared the finish might be in sight. Late September was targetted for final inspection, cleaning and moving furniture in, with a target date of mid-October for the first service back. How appropriate—that would be right around Thanksgiving and the church anniversary!

In Phase 2 there were several improvements made to the former structure as the board re-examined the past setup and looked ahead to what would be coming in Phase 3. A partial list of those changes should suffice to demonstrate how this building effort was considered the final major one for the facility on this site—the goal was to get everything as right as possible: the sound booth was enlarged to facilitate an expanded audio and video ministry; an audio loop was installed beneath the carpet and pews of the main auditorium to allow for much improved hearing assistance throughout the room; the pathway from the narthex to the new building would now run a straight path—this necessitated a shifting of the base of the stairs to the balcony, a change to the cloak room and a reduction in the space that had once been in front of the nursery; two washrooms would be added along the east wall of that corridor in the next phase; all the holes dug into the lower auditorium floor (made when the search for the mysterious oil pathway was at its height) were filled and a new floor installed; with fuel oil now identified as Public Enemy #1, the old furnaces were replaced with propane ones, with a new storage tank installed behind the church building; everything up and downstairs was given a fresh coat of paint and the doors were ready to open.

Back home at last!

As restoration work on the 2004 building was being completed, a day was set aside in which all items that had been removed, cleaned and stored would be returned to the church building. Saturday, September 28, 2019, was a watershed moment in the whole restoration project as it signalled an initial return to the building that had been vacated just over two years earlier. In the days immediately following the fire, no one had expected the process to be so lengthy or so costly. However, even with the alterations, the essential elements of the building were the same; no one was going to get lost or disoriented. The church anniversary services were held at St. George's and Ebenezer on the first weekend in October (earlier than normal to facilitate the schedule of the guest speaker, Dr. Joel Beeke). Then, after a couple of hopeful false starts, the long-awaited email was finally sent out announcing the church building had cleared the final approval hurdle and would be open for occupation!

Sunday, October 27, 2019, 802 days after fire struck the church, the congregation rejoiced to be back home! There was a celebratory fellowship hour prior to the morning service, allowing people to see what had been done and to get an idea of the work remaining to get the facility entirely operational. The usable areas were all within the 2004 addition and included the main auditorium, narthex, washroom and office upstairs, and the fellowship hall, washrooms and kitchen downstairs. The elevator was also in service. With access to the south parking area limited by the remaining fencing around the area of future construction, a valet parking service was set up for those who found it difficult to walk from the north lot. This allowed a drop-off and pick-up area in the south lot where a temporary sidewalk provided access to the main entrance without the need to climb steps; a blessing to those who found steps a challenging obstacle. In the fellowship hall, dividers were used to create space for a temporary nursery and for Sunday School classes, which began again in earnest the first week in November.

In Carl's first message that morning, he outlined six lessons he and the congregation had learned during the twenty-six months of pilgrimage. The main theme centred on issues that were always of primary importance to the congregation and indicative of the Lord's character, whether meeting on Appleby Line or elsewhere.

1. God's great concern for souls.
2. God's great provision is people (especially the Lord Jesus).
3. God's great plan is our godliness.
4. God's great emphasis is dependence.
5. God's great blessing is providence.
6. God's great example is love, for both saint and sinner.

With these lessons learned, along with countless others, the challenge was now to go out and live for His glory, individually and as a body of believers. It was fitting that this message was the first to be streamed live through Sermon Audio.

Phase 3

The final permits for Phase 3, the new structure on the 1890 site, were finally granted at the end of November 2019, and the work began the first week of December! Progress was immediate and the foundations and basement walls were soon complete. It was a good time to remind the congregation that the building was being built for God's purposes. In an email to the church, elder Harry Droogendyk, who had been fulfilling the extensive duties of project manager for many months, said,

> We are very thankful for God's mercy in how He's worked through appraisers, adjusters and construction contractors to orchestrate the mundane financial bits and to protect Trinity's fiscal health and ensure our ministry efforts at home and abroad were not compromised because of the fire. Trinity Baptist Church is not a club that exists for its own comfort. We've been saved and placed within the context of this local body so this body might be the hands, feet and voice of a gracious God in this world that so desperately needs Christ and His grace. We cannot overstate the wonder of God's providence in how He's worked all this out! We anticipate ministering in a building where virtually everything is new or renewed, with additional capability, while retaining the capacity to be used of God as He works in Burlington and across the world—we are very thankful for God's care of our church.

A constant prayer of people at Trinity was that they would always be found faithful in the proclamation of the gospel, standing for God's truth and returning praise and thanksgiving for blessings enjoyed without measure. As the decade closed, the church family looked forward to the joys of another Christmas season rejoicing at the coming of the Son of God into the world. They understood what Christ was telling his disciples in Luke 10:20, "rejoice because your names are written in heaven" (NKJV). That was the key to real joy—to have one's name written in the Lamb's Book of Life![12] What a great privilege to be children of the living God!

---

[12] Revelation 21:27.

7

Winding up the first half-century

2020–2022

Associate pastoral role revived

Carl Muller was an assistant pastor for the final years of Pastor Payne's ministry. The elders were led to recommend to the board and then the church family that this position be examined once again. There was a young man in the church who was attending TBS, who showed real promise in terms of preaching and had shown a high level of faithfulness in attendance and participation in church ministries. Josh Mills had preached on a number of occasions and had been a blessing to the congregation.

Carl had presented to the elders his intention to retire from full time ministry after he turned sixty-five in Fall 2022. There had been some general discussion about how that transition could or should take place. In a letter sent to the congregation the first week of March 2020, an outline was presented for moving forward in terms of pastoral leadership. Portions of that letter are included here to demonstrate the importance of this position in the life of the church and the key elements of the ministry to which the associate would attend.

Overview
For some time now the elders have been exploring the feasibility and practicality of going a step beyond our internship program (which we hope to see continue in the future) and bringing on an associate pastor to assist with the work in the church. The chief reasons are as follows:

1. There are limits to how much time and energy any pastor can give to a work and we feel Carl has been operating at that limit for some time.
2. As was the case with Pastor Payne, Carl has been given more and more opportunities to minister to groups beyond Trinity. His experience and wisdom, developed through years of faithful service, have equipped him to help train and develop men in situations far afield. To do this properly requires time. It was one of the main reasons Carl came on as assistant to Pastor Payne later in his ministry.
3. There are aspects of ministry within the church that have not received the attention they deserve due to lack of available pastoral hours.
4. We are still very committed to the training of younger men for the ministry and believe a longer term of service in pastoral work (i.e., beyond the four-month intern period) could be of tremendous benefit to a successful candidate.

We believe the addition of an associate pastor would be of noticeable benefit in all these areas. The individual under consideration as a candidate is Josh Mills, who, we believe, has demonstrated a clear equipping by God for work in the ministry. He has the full support of the entire board, having already been a blessing in so many ways in his time with us.

The role of the associate pastor
It is not easy to lay out the weekly schedule for an individual in pastoral work as numerous events can arise with little or no notice that require the pastor to rearrange that schedule. It is possible, however, to at least lay out specific responsibilities that could be reasonably expected within the role of associate. As the finances section outlines, we would be looking to hire the associate on a part-time basis, 24 hours per week. The list of duties below is not exhaustive but will easily fill up 24 hours in a week.

1. Preach at least twice each month, filling in at other times when needed.
2. Take a regular turn teaching the adult Sunday School class.
3. Take the teaching lead at Wednesday evening prayer meetings.
4. Participate in all meetings and take on all the duties of an elder.
5. Take the lead in developing and pursuing an outreach to the neighbourhood.
6. Meet with the pastor on a regular basis for discussion, feedback and prayer.
7. Pursue a regimen of regular reading of books, articles, etc in consultation with the pastor.
8. Assist in visitation.

An associate could be of inestimable help on many fronts. We believe that the Trinity church family would be the beneficiaries of blessing as a result.

Finances
There are still some uncertainties with respect to final building costs, though things are progressing smoothly, as evidenced by the ongoing construction of the new building. There may yet be a need to borrow some money to see that all the upgrades are satisfactorily included, but that overall amount, we hope, will be quite manageable.

In light of that reality, the board would like to keep any additional costs connected to taking on an associate at this time within practical reason. The proposal then would include the following specifics:

1. Offer only part-time employment at this time, totaling 24 hours/week, at a rate of $20/hr.
2. The contract would run for 17 months, starting May 1, 2020 and ending Sept. 30, 2021.

Even with some past items coming off the books in the next budget, there would still be an increase in overall expense; giving would have to be increased by the congregation in order to cover it. The people of Trinity have always risen to the challenge brought on by new ventures that they believe honour the Lord and are of spiritual and practical benefit to His people. We trust that would be the case in this instance.[1]

The plan, at the time, was to pursue the following steps:

1. In early March inform the members (via letter) of the proposal to hire an associate. This will include a clear outline of the associated financial realities, as well as the rationale for this change at the present time.
2. Call a church meeting for Wednesday, April 1st for a time of Q&A on the proposal. This will also be a time for members to ask questions of Josh.
3. On Wednesday, April 22nd (the usual meeting to vote on church officers) the members would be asked to vote on (i) the proposal for an associate pastor position, and, if passed, (ii) on Josh as our candidate for that position for the stated 17-month period of service.
4. At the conclusion of that period (Sept. 30, 2021) the situation would be reassessed, and recommendations made to (i) continue with the same specifications of employment, (ii) make alterations to the parameters of employment, or (iii) end the contract at that point, all to be based on church circumstances at the time.

If Josh is a successful candidate for associate pastor it should be noted that he would be received by the membership in the role of church elder as well.[2]

---

[1] Trinity Baptist Church, letter to the congregation, March 2020.
[2] Trinity Baptist Church, letter to the congregation, March 2020.

Seeds were also planted regarding Carl's anticipated retirement in Fall 2022. To that end some general ideas were shared with the congregation.

> *Slightly more-distant future*
> Not everything goes on as it has forever; even pastors grow a little older over time. Carl has informed the board that he plans to retire from full-time ministry when he turns 65, in September 2022. In preparation for that time of transition please know that, at the appropriate lead-up time to that date, the elders, acting in their role as pastoral search committee, would initiate a plan to search for a new man to step into the role Carl would have held for 25 years at that point. God has been gracious in giving us faithful men to take the lead in preaching and teaching and we are trusting Him to give us His man for our need at that time. Please commit these matters to prayer. We want to do what the Lord sees as best for us, both now and in the future.[3]

Of course, with even the best laid and most detailed plans, there can be unseen rocks in the stream. With Covid-19 restrictions, these meetings in April could not be held. Instead, Josh was taken on in the traditional intern role, which had already been approved by the members in the previous budget. It was revisited in the fall, at the annual general business meeting. At that September meeting, both the proposal for an associate pastor and Josh Mills to fill that position were readily accepted by the members, and Josh joined the board as elder and associate pastor. In due course, he would also take on the responsibilities of administrative assistant—a position many pastors like to see in the hands of others.

Insurance issues

Even though it had been over two years since the fire, work on repairing the damage continued. The amount of time spent by men on the board overseeing this work has not been calculated, but it had been a colossal undertaking for those involved. One of the great challenges was tracking the money going back and forth among the insurers, the tradespeople, the engineers, various government offices and the church. The treasurer had

---

[3] Trinity Baptist Church, letter to the congregation, March 2020.

to run a second set of financial figures, apart from the regular monthly and annual financial statements for the church, to identify what was fire related and what was not. The insurers were responsible for paying their portion of invoices while the church had to calculate their share of the HST and pay it directly; then, of course, make application to the CRA[4] twice a year to recoup that expense. The record keeping had to be meticulous, and that portion under the control of the church certainly was. That couldn't always be said for those submitting invoices and the insurer's reliability in seeing they were paid in the correct amounts and on time. Some details regarding the replacement of contents lost due to the fire were not finally hammered out until thirty months on. In spite of the delays, recalculations, resubmissions and innumerable emails, phone calls and meetings, the final cheque from the insurers was finally issued in early 2021. The total cost of the cleanup, repair and reconstruction was around the $3-million mark. The majority was covered by the insurers, though the church contributed a couple of hundred thousand to deal with upgrades to make the entire facility better in many ways.

Ministry rekindled

As the new decade opened, the church enjoyed the excitement of getting back to some regular programs of ministry. Sunday School was operational, though still modified for several classes due to ongoing facility limitations, as was Kids Club. A men's breakfast was held the first week of February and was well attended with over forty men and boys present to hear a message from Pastor Hagop Tchobanian from Pilgrim Baptist Fellowship, Hamilton. By the third week of February, the new building had been framed and crowned with roof trusses. With the overall shape and various dimensions being more visible, it was possible to imagine occupying and utilizing the new space soon. With the rebuild underway there was a great sense of optimism within the congregation that 2020 would be a year of stabilization and growth after travelling the many sideroads down which the Lord had taken them. The Lord, however, had His own agenda and plans whose nature and scope would have drastic and unexpected effects on Trinity and the entire world. He reminded everyone of the words of Isaiah,

---

[4] Canada Revenue Agency.

"Remember this and stand firm,
   recall it to mind, you transgressors,
   remember the former things of old;
for I am God, and there is no other;
   I am God, and there is none like me,
declaring the end from the beginning
   and from ancient times things not yet done,
saying, 'My counsel shall stand,
   and I will accomplish all my purpose,'
calling a bird of prey from the east,
   the man of my counsel from a far country.
I have spoken, and I will bring it to pass;
   I have purposed, and I will do it" (Isaiah 46:8–11 ESV).

An infection goes viral ... literally!

Covid-19

Early in January 2020, news began to emerge of a new virus spreading rapidly in one specific province in China. Coronavirus disease 2019 (Covid-19—"co" for *corona*, "vi" for *virus* and "d" for *disease*, with "19" as the year of discovery) was an infectious disease caused by severe acute respiratory syndrome coronavirus 2 (SARS-CoV-2). The disease was first identified in late 2019 in Wuhan, the capital of Hubei province in central China, and soon spread globally, resulting in the 2019–2022 coronavirus pandemic. Its final impact on the world, physically, emotionally and economically, was without precedent in recent history. SARS, first seen in 2002–2003, and MERS in 2012 had an impact, but nothing, since the Spanish Influenza outbreak in 1918–1920 that killed up to 50 million people worldwide, had roiled the world like this. As nations and localities attempted to contain the spread of the virus, extraordinary protocols were introduced and enforced. Travel was severely restricted, especially for those individuals coming from countries with the highest early rates of infection. Social distancing (generally accepted as 2 metres or 6 feet) was a term introduced as an exhortation to allow space and avoid close contagious contact with others. Society was introduced to the goal of "flattening the curve," which meant preventing a huge spike in cases that could overwhelm the ability of hospitals to handle them all, and to spread the number of infected patients out over time. Anyone returning from outside the country was required to self-isolate (not going anywhere for any reason) for fourteen days (the generally accepted time of a person being infectious after contracting the illness), with the possibility of fines, or worse, for those who didn't comply. Virtually all sporting and arts events, anything that would normally see crowds of people in confined spaces, were cancelled. The National Basketball Association (NBA), National Hockey League (NHL), European soccer, the spring season for all university sports, parades, concerts—all shut down. Even the Olympic Summer Games planned for Tokyo in July 2020 were postponed and rescheduled for the following year. Initially, elementary, secondary and post-secondary schools, were to be closed for at least two weeks after the traditional March break, though that timeframe was extended in mid-April throughout Ontario to at least the start of May, and ended up running to the end of the academic year in June. Students, teachers and parents had to quickly adapt to a variety of online teaching/learning methods as the thought of losing the entire spring of school became a potential reality. Libraries, recreation centres, art galleries, museums, welcome centres, movie theatres, camps—all closed. With groups of only five allowed to gather for inside meetings, many churches and other places of worship resorted to broadcasting services and messages online.

The economic impact ramped up quickly, as restrictions increased. With the travel and tourism industry largely put on hold (restaurants and bars closed, hotels were mostly empty, airlines cancelled hundreds of flights, most tourist attractions closed) millions of workers worldwide were laid off. Canada's federal and provincial governments scrambled to find ways to help offset the salary hit even as employment insurance (EI) claims skyrocketed, soon passing the million plateau. Tens of billions of dollars of relief for businesses were under review, as financial markets continued to freefall with a potential worldwide recession (or depression) hovering on the horizon. Facing the unknown, and one that was as scary as this, led to panic among some and some irrational behaviour. Perhaps the most noticeable was that of the mass purchasing of hand sanitizer, medical masks and toilet paper. In the first few weeks, paper product shelves in stores were almost always empty, as families stocked up on what they saw as the greatest essentials. Pasta and other dried foods were often in short supply, though the grocery stores did an excellent job keeping most necessities in stock despite the challenges in the food delivery chain.

As in all emergency situations, frontline workers were at greatest risk of infection or injury. Some areas had adequate personal protection equipment

(PPE) on hand but there was, in the early stages, not enough to go around. A medical mobilization on an unmatched scale was implemented to stem the tide of infections. Testing got faster and new cases identified more efficiently. One of the biggest challenges was the spread caused by those who were infected, but showed no symptoms; there was a tendency for those individuals to feel safe to be around others, thinking they could do no harm.

At the same time, there was also a significant number of people who believed the entire pandemic to be largely overblown and the restrictions quite unnecessary. Published numbers of infections, serious illness and deaths related to Covid-19 were regularly disputed, the science behind those numbers seriously doubted, with the overarching charge of conspiracy on a number of fronts always being presented with energy, determination and supportive arguments from alternate sources. Some believed governments were pursuing agendas not in the best interest of the citizenry, the medical establishment was in the pocket of the government, Covid had been created and spread on purpose by either the Chinese or American government. Perhaps time will reveal if any or all of these counter positions were indeed accurate. At the very least, a sense of mistrust of those offering both details and solutions was growing in some quarters.

At first, a given percentage of room capacity dictated how many people could meet. At 50 per cent, all those who desired to come to Trinity were able to meet weekly. Many of the elderly and those who were ill generally opted to join the service online. With increased restrictions, that number started to shrink even more and was eventually replaced with raw totals, such as a limit of ten or five people. As a result of the numbers able to attend dropping, Trinity moved almost exclusively to an online service on March 22, 2020. Pastor Muller preached to an almost empty auditorium, but was live-streamed to the congregation which was able to watch using Sermon Audio live feed or listen to the audio version through their phones. For the March 29th service, with a message and prayer again delivered to a reduced congregation, the ability to watch the live feed was limited by technical challenges. With virtually all churches closed, the number of people at home utilizing Sermon Audio as a feed for their services was immense and the demand overran its capacity to deliver. As a result, it wasn't possible for everyone to get access to the live feed and they had to resort to audio only. The good news was the Trinity congregation knew exactly what Carl looked like and simply pictured him there at the pulpit as they listened to his voice.

Prayer meetings still went ahead, as the numbers attending were within the guidelines, and proper social distancing could be employed. Most other programs and special events were either cancelled or put on hold. Some of the cancellations in March included Camp Courageous, the visiting TBS team and the annual missions conference. Kids Club was suspended indefinitely, as was the Sunday School program, and the special missions offering was postponed. However, for the well-being of the church, the members still had to offer input (albeit from a distance) on important decisions regarding the future.

As already noted, a proposal from the board to the membership, on the possible hiring of an associate pastor was distributed on March 11th. It included the rationale for the position, the term of the contract, total hours and remuneration, general job description as well as a timetable for prayerful consideration, a public Q&A and a vote in late April. Not being allowed to meet, however, changed these plans. Thus, the shift to bringing Josh Mills on as intern for the summer months.

Pastor Carl's message on March 22, 2020, focused on Romans 8:28–30, emphasizing the fact that, even in difficult times for the church and for the nation, God is always working. He used the key elements of the passage to encourage and strengthen the congregation.

Main points:
1. God is working out His holy will—even, and always, in a troubled world.
2. God is working to save souls—this is always His major agenda in the working out of His will.
3. God is working and is unstoppable—the church will be built, and the kingdom will come.
4. God is working, and He uses means—He uses us, and He uses circumstances.

Implications and challenges:
1. Will you pray?—for basic needs but especially for salvation.
2. Will you speak?—will you take our present circumstances and use them as opportunities to share the gospel?
3. Will you be confident?—that God is sovereign and hence we need not fear.

4. Will you ask the awkward question?—is this pandemic a judgement from God?[5]

From what was transpiring in the world at the time, it was apparent a growing level of fear and anxiety was gripping the nations. This was a God-given opportunity to display a spirit of peace, calm and ultimate trust in the heavenly Father to continue to do all things well.

As efforts to contain the virus and minimize its overall impact continued to evolve, the number of people allowed to meet together in Ontario hit rock-bottom at five. This meant live-streaming a service would only allow Pastor Carl, two video technicians, a musician and one other person to gather at the church for the broadcast. To encourage singing, taped versions of hymns were broadcast with the words so people could join in at home. Group restrictions also put a complete stop to prayer meetings at the church. However, utilizing the Zoom app (along with multitudes around the world), the first virtual prayer meeting was held on March 25, 2020, with seventeen households connecting (about twenty-five people in total) for prayer. A few technical glitches had to be overcome, but Zoom meetings became the norm for the next number of weeks as the church family awaited the opportunity to gather once again. These sessions allowed for some much-needed face to face connection, at least for those who were able to join in. Friends also joined from outside Ontario, with connections from both Manitoba and New Zealand!

These overriding provincial regulations also halted construction at the church for a while, as it was considered to be "non-essential" work. Brouwer Construction worked quickly to seal up the building as tightly as possible, even showing up on the first Saturday in April to raise the steeple, finish the roof framing and close in the window openings. The work stoppage was brief, thankfully, and they resumed their excellent progress when they were allowed to restart work during the third week of May. The lower portions of the windows were soon installed though the curved top sections didn't arrive until a few weeks later. This at least allowed some of the interior work to proceed without further concern for inclement weather.

---

[5] Carl Muller, "What is God doing in the world?"; see https://www.sermonaudio.com/sermon/32120200356904.

Even something as simple as taking up an offering was displaced. Though prayers of thankfulness for God's goodness to the church remained a part of the regular service, a system of electronic giving was introduced for those who chose that route. Most of the congregation were comfortable with e-transfers and overall giving remained stable. Those who still preferred the more visible means of cheques or cash were accommodated. Seamlessly weaving the giving, the entering of those gifts into the church financial records and the issuing of charitable receipts at the end of the year was accomplished by those with the appropriate technical acumen. It all ran quite smoothly and the people gave generously and in a timely manner, just as they always had.

Having already been physically displaced for over two years, the congregation at Trinity Baptist Church continued to show tremendous resiliency in being displaced once again. This time, however, the whole Christian world was dealing with exactly the same issue and there was a measure of comfort in that. Good Friday and Easter Sunday were, for the first time in most people's lives, being remembered and celebrated virtually, and the Word was still preached. In a note to the congregation, elder Harry Droogendyk shared the following comments for their encouragement:

> Please be much in prayer for this weekend. Our world is a troubled place and people have been shaken by the Covid-19 hysteria. We know of three or four unchurched families who have asked how they might be able to join our online services. Of course, Easter is often a time when some make their annual visit for the sake of tradition, but in these cases, it seems the Lord is using the current events to stir up a hunger for certainty and foundations that cannot be moved. There's been more evidence of that across the world. Many churches are reporting that their online services have more participants than normally attend on the Lord's Day. Let us pray the Lord might revive His church and send a great awakening into this poor sin-sick world which needs Christ so desperately. Pray also for pastors who will be preaching from their studies or to empty buildings. Pray for audio / video technicians who must sometimes deal with ornery software and feel the pressure of hundreds of viewing eyes.[6]

---

[6] Trinity Baptist Church, note to the congregation, April 2020.

With the on and off again ability to meet at the church, the usual distribution of bulletins was not practical. In April 2020, the elders began to send out to the church family, via Google Groups, a weekly document entitled "Notes from the Elders." They presented a brief meditation from the pastor, items for prayer and praise, mission prayer points, a rotating list of people from the church for whom to pray, an item on the persecuted church, updates, announcements and some helpful online resources. The purpose was to keep the congregation, scattered by physical distance, focusing on common themes and lessons on a regular basis. When face to face was not possible, the *Notes* were at least a channel of encouragement, instruction and connectivity.

Online services and Zoom prayer meetings were the norm until the Hamilton and Halton areas moved into what became known in Ontario as Phase 2, of three proposed phases for emergence from lockdown. Most important to the people of Trinity was the reopening of churches for gathered worship. There were restrictions, of course, but even sticking to the 30 per cent building capacity permitted, it allowed up to 120 people into the church building. The new restrictions went into effect on Friday, June 12, 2020, and the first service back in the building was held Sunday, June 14. People met for morning and evening services with the usual protocols in place, carefully laid out by the deacons and elders and communicated to the people beforehand. Alternating pews were closed off, family groups or individuals were spaced the widely publicized six feet apart, as seating was overseen by ushers from the front pews to the back. Words for singing were on the screen, though the congregation remained seated while they sang. Not everyone felt safe coming into a group environment that first week, or for many weeks after; many of the elderly continued to stay away, as did some others who felt the risk of a Covid-19 infection was just too great. Masking was not required in the first weeks, though some rumblings about compulsory face masks in all public places were occurring in other locales across the country and within the province. Prayer meeting returned to the church building on June 10, 2020, though a Zoom add-on was included to allow families to join in from home. This hybrid meeting was considered a successful beginning and, with some slight alterations, became another new norm for a while.

The Lord's table, which had not been served since the lockdown, was reintroduced on June 21, 2020, as part of the morning service. With so many restrictions still in place, a process needed to be established to allow believers to participate while adhering as much as possible to provincial guidelines. The solution was found in a pre-packaged "Fellowship Cup"—consisting of a sealed cup of juice (very much like a coffee creamer) with a soft wafer wrapped and attached to the top. Anyone planning to participate picked this small package up as they entered the auditorium and then utilized the contents appropriately as the Lord's table took on its traditional form of singing, Scripture reading and prayer. Where there was a will there was a way!

With fear of a second wave rampant (highly publicized and stoked by the news media), many communities opted for a compulsory masking in indoor public spaces. So, beginning at prayer meeting on Wednesday, July 22nd, and continuing with the services on Sunday, July 26th, face masks were to worn by those entering the church building. Mask wearing was practiced by some but not all, and that seemed to be an ongoing issue for some but not most. The singing may have been a little muted, but was robust nonetheless. The number of Covid cases remained reasonably low in the local communities, though this kind of a precaution was part of an effort to try and keep it that way. It was hard at times to see who was taking it with a smile, with all those masks in the way.

Key events, usually popular with different groups from the church, were cancelled: SGF youth, ladies and pastors retreats, and, for the first time in over forty years, the Canadian Carey Family Conference. The fellowship and Christian growth engendered by these events were greatly missed by those across the Reformed spectrum of churches in Southern Ontario.

The Covid saga droned on through at least four waves of spiking infections and hospital admissions, with dire worst-case scenarios shared through the media daily, amid a roller-coaster of shifting announcements of what was recommended by the medical field and some scientists. Even though the worst cases never materialized, there was significant strain placed on the medical system, with innumerable cancellations of elective surgeries and tremendous emotional and physical wear and tear on frontline nurses and caregivers in particular. The hardest hit population was the elderly, many of whom were not physically able to fight off the infections, often due to underlying physical weaknesses in other areas. Some long-term care facilities saw many of their residents succumb to this illness. Though the actual numbers of infections and deaths across all spectrums were probably exaggerated in some arenas, the impact of Covid-19 on Canada and the world was still enormously significant. The long-term fallout and hidden costs to the economic, physical, emotional and spiritual health of so many will only be revealed over time.

The Lord's testing by trial

As the fiftieth anniversary approached, it appeared the final couple of years would probably just be a brief historical epilogue, stating that all was well on the home front, people continued to grow in grace and the knowledge of the Lord Jesus, the unity continued unabated and the church grew and prospered right up to, and through, its Year of Jubilee. God's providences and plans, however, do not always lead to such a sweet finale in the life of a church. There was, sadly, to be one final rending of the fabric of Trinity at the eleventh hour. The church was about to be divided, with a suddenness and finality that no one could have expected.

There were a number of issues being hotly debated in the public forum, as well as in church circles in the early part of the 2020s. Some, such as abortion, gay marriage, women in leadership and worship styles in the church, had already been discussed for some time; yet they were still able to generate a fine discourse among believers when raised. More recent issues—such as Black Lives Matter, Truth and Reconciliation for Indigenous People, Critical Race Theory (CRT), gender dysphoria and related gender concerns—vigorously pushed themselves to the front of the line and were in a constant state of dialogue/debate/discussion/dispute/disagreement. Churches found themselves pulled in different directions by the strongly held convictions of their own members and adherents, some of which were based on various biblical arguments, but many based solely on social justice perspectives. One of the most invasive issues, however, was the change in society brought about by Covid-19 and the debate over how best to respond to it. The impact on the general population was profound, and no less so within evangelical churches. Trinity was not exempt from some of the fallout.

The events that unfolded at Trinity Baptist Church between late 2020 and early 2021 seemed to arise from a variety of overlying and intertwined factors. The complexity of attempting to piece together everything that occurred in that timeframe, with precision and proper balance, was a task beyond the ability of this writer, as it became impossible to accurately reflect all the intentions and purposes of those involved. Interpretation can be an inaccurate science at the best of times. Memory can be another area that presents a murkiness often difficult to pin down with confidence. What was said, what was meant, what was heard, what was concluded, what was left in, what was left out, what was emphasized, what was minimized—these are not easily unravelled, yet all played a significant role in eventual outcomes. Undoubtedly, emotions had their own part to play, as did personal convictions, perspectives and priorities. As a result, the events and outcomes will be presented in very brief format. The intention is not to reopen wounds and relive hurts experienced by many in the congregation, especially within the leadership.

In the new year, Pastor Carl took an extended leave from ministry, eventually stretching from January 2021 to a potential return in May 2021. As he was away, much of the preaching responsibility fell to associate pastor Josh Mills, who filled in admirably under the circumstances. However, just prior to pastor Carl's return, matters of concern on various issues were raised and presented, with some discussion, at two board meetings that took place in late April 2021. By the end of those meetings, four elders had resigned from their positions, including Pastor Carl. Over the next two months, efforts were made to resolve issues of difference and create a clear path forward. However, little progress was made in bridging the gaps that existed. So, on Wednesday, June 16th, a members meeting was held in the parking lot of the church so everyone who wanted could attend.

The congregation had received a number of documents intended to give background and clarity on how events had unfolded and brought the church to their present position. Members were invited to ask questions and hear answers from those holding differing positions. It was a difficult meeting. As a result of all the events leading up to this point, in the days after the meeting a number of families and individuals submitted their membership resignations, including Pastor Carl. The majority of members remained as part of Trinity.

Many of those who chose to leave, soon banded together with the desire to continue meeting as a group, with Carl taking the lead in terms of preaching. In a relatively short period, they formed a new congregation, eventually voting in Carl as pastor, along with two other elders and three deacons. They met regularly as a congregation and set about looking for the Lord's guidance and blessing as they sought to move forward in His service as Providence Baptist Church.

At Trinity, there was an immediate need to reestablish a broader base of spiritual leadership and not leave Pastor Josh on his own as the sole elder. Later in the summer, nominations for elder were held and, after a church vote, the initial two elders who had resigned were reinstated with the blessing of the congregation, each displaying the desire to serve the church. The Trinity congregation was looking to the Lord for sustaining grace and His hand of blessing on their plans going forward. In the end, one church family had become two.

Ultimately, the events that led to the present state of things at Trinity were not foreseen or planned by any in the congregation. God's plans are certainly not always laid out for us to see or even completely understand. However, in the hands of the sovereign Lord, good would still come out of all that had happened and it would, as always, result in His honour and glory and the good of His people.

The rebuild finally completed

With delays due to Covid-19 and delays with some supply items, the work on the building proceeded in stops and starts throughout 2020. The company hired to do the build were dependable and did their work well. Foundations, floors, walls, rafters, roof, windows, stone and brick work, rough-ins, electrical, plumbing, heating, drywall and painting were all done, and step by step the building came together. The people rejoiced to see the progress and longed for the day when programs could once again make full use of the building the Lord had given for ministry. As always, it would happen in the Lord's good time!

Then, after hundreds of hours of labour, and just as many decisions made, the work on the rebuild was completed in the final week of June 2021. The church facility was now practically brand new in all areas. The new fellowship hall in the rebuilt 1890 wing has proved wonderfully useful as a multipurpose facility. The kitchen that was added allowed for smaller groups to enjoy food and fellowship without having to resort to the big space downstairs. The library was reimagined and books were once again filling the shelves. Classroom space was much appreciated by those who used it, especially those who could remember the interesting labyrinth of rooms that had once been the downstairs realm. The additional features added over and above the insurance coverage, made for better use of space, better access and egress from all parts of the facility, a more useful set of technical tools and options that better fitted the twenty-first century, more convenient access to washroom facilities and much improved movement

The new section of Trinity Baptist Church on the footprint of the 1890 church

Photo © Henry van Zanden

within the building. With the previous insurance policy somewhat used up, the board wisely increased the new coverage to deal with present day financial realities and costs. The beauty and utility of the overall facility is a blessing to the entire congregation. The Lord again was to be praised for His oversight of the entire project.

The fiftieth year

Starting in September 2021, the church appointed Josh as lead pastor. The newly rebuilt board was hard at work re-establishing all aspects of ministry, and contacts continued to be made with people in the congregations' spheres of influence. As a result, and in the Lord's kindness, there was an influx of new families and individuals, as well as a number of people who decided to pursue baptism and church membership. In early December 2021, the church celebrated the baptism of nine candidates, and added almost a dozen others as members. An additional two baptisms and eleven new members came on board in June 2022. The testimony time, as always, was a tremendous blessing to all in attendance. These public testimonies, in both word and deed, pointed everyone once again to the God of salvation and the Saviour Himself, the Lord Jesus Christ. After such a challenging spring, these were lovely gifts from the Lord with which to fill out Trinity's fiftieth year.

During the first part of 2022, the church continued with its weekly ministries, including a dedicated week of prayer and fasting, often drawing forty to fifty people each night. This was a corporate time to ask for the Lord's blessing, direction and sustaining grace and mercy. Much prayer was sent heavenward for the salvation of the lost, the ongoing equipping of the saints, the sanctification of all believers, as well as a plea for a great moving of the Holy Spirit locally, nationally and internationally. The need for a great spiritual awakening was deeply felt. Healing was requested for the sick and comfort for those sorrowing or grieving.

The church members were also much in prayer for Pastor Josh and his wife Kyla. They discovered early on in her pregnancy that their child was dealing with a defective area of his heart. The prognosis was not good, especially if he were to be born prematurely. Josh and Kyla immediately and regularly took their concerns to the Lord and He sustained them wonderfully and graciously through myriads of appointments and seemingly never-ending decisions. Many prayers were offered by members of the congregation and friends and family far and wide for their well-being and the possible healing of their young son. After his birth, Isaac lived twelve days, days in which he was loved and embraced by his mom and dad and some close family members. The Lord, in His infinite wisdom, took Isaac from this world, but not before he had made a lifelong impact on any who knew him or heard about him. The Lord was kind to Trinity during that challenging time as well, by providing a regular feast on the Word with the men who filled in while Josh was set aside for his family's needs.

Most of the time, of course, the people at Trinity were busily engaged in doing what churches do: seeking to faithfully preach and teach the gospel of Jesus, set the eyes of the people on God while exhorting them to know Him better, ministering to the various needs of the people, calling the lost to salvation and striving to live a consistently spiritual life before family, colleagues, neighbours and friends. Their ongoing task was to labour on for the Lord that He might be glorified in all things. The broad range of church ministries was reawakened with the reestablishing of Sunday School for all ages, College & Careers, Kids Club (up to 20 in attendance), biweekly ladies Bible study, quarterly men's breakfasts and monthly men's prayer meetings. Efforts were made to reconnect with the entire spectrum of the church body. To allow for greater communion with other believers, a weekly fellowship hour after the morning service was begun. It has been well attended and much appreciated. Not just looking inward, the church also increased its presence with outside community ministries, especially a Friday night evangelism program involving other churches.

God has been gracious in many ways. There is a broadly expressed awareness and hearty acknowledgement of a wonderful spirit of unity in the closing months of the fiftieth year. Members of the congregation want to be involved and be of service to the Lord and to His people. There has been much thanksgiving for the Lord's mercy and kindness in all He has done. There is bright hope for the future, as God continues to build His church overall and His local church on Appleby Line in particular. By God's grace, the congregation will continue to serve for as long as He is pleased to maintain and uphold this body of believers known collectively as Trinity Baptist Church.

With the number of logistical requirements that go into publishing a book, it is not possible to make a record right up to the fiftieth anniversary weekend. There was a cut-off point, a deadline so to speak, that would allow these historical notes to come to light. Therefore, this account will only cover as far as the end of June 2022.

Trinity Baptist Church, Burlington, Ont., November 2021
Photo © Henry van Zanden

The final word appropriately goes to Pastor Josh, the lead pastor as this half century comes to a close and the next begins. It is a reflection on the past and a hopeful look to the future.

> From its inception to the present day, Trinity Baptist Church has sought to declare the whole counsel of God (Acts 20:27), holding to the primacy of Jesus Christ for all of life, praying in the power of the Spirit for the edification of the saints and the salvation of sinners.
>
> As we look forward to the future, I am reminded of the words of R.C. Sproul: "Every generation needs to recover anew the Word of God and rely on its power afresh." Today, we find ourselves in dark days. However, the task remains the same. In the coming years, we must rely upon the power of the Word of God afresh and proclaim the Word of God from the pulpit to the pew, and from the pew to the community, and then, from the community to the nations, that God may be glorified in the salvation of sinners! In light of this, here are specific prayer requests going forward for Trinity Baptist Church:
>
> 1. May the subject of the ministry of Trinity Baptist Church, as long as it stands, always be the person and work of our Lord Jesus Christ.
> 2. May we grow in our hospitality and fellowship, and love for one another, earnestly seeking to welcome one another as Christ has welcomed us (Romans 15:7).
> 3. May we be equipped "for the work of ministry, for building up the body of Christ, until we all attain to the unity of the faith and of the knowledge of the Son of God, to mature manhood, to the measure of the stature of the fullness of Christ" (Ephesians 4:12–13 ESV).
>
> To Him alone be all glory (Romans 11:36). Amen.
>
> *Josh Mills*
> *Pastor, Trinity Baptist Church*
> *March 31, 2022*

Josh & Kyla Mills with their son Isaac

Appendix 1

Founding members of Trinity Baptist Church

Audrey Brouwers
Mrs. J. Brouwers
Mr. J. Brouwers
Mrs. Jan Brouwers
Mr. Jan Brouwers
Mrs. H. Clarke
Mr. H. Clarke
Mrs. R. Clarke
Mr. R. Clarke
Steven Clarke
Russell Clarke

Mrs. R. Duez
Mr. R. Duez
Mrs. J. Haughie
Mr. J. Haughie
Brian Haughie
Mr. B. Langford
Mrs. D. Leggett
Mr. D. Leggett
Pat McMahon
Mrs. Wm. Payne
Rev. Wm. Payne

Marjorie Pearce
Barbara Redman
Mrs. R. Schaub
Mr. R. Schaub
Mrs. C. Wellum
Dr. C. Wellum
Mrs. R. Wilkins
Mr. R. Wilkins
Mrs. D. Wilson
Mr. D. Wilson

Appendix 2

Key positions of service & leadership

◇◇◇◇◇◇◇◇◇

These lists show the names of those holding key positions of service and leadership. Not all those who served in these ministries are included, as written records were sometimes sparse (especially in the early years) and usually just showed those who took the main lead; these workers were identified through published ministry lists, annual reports and notes in the bulletin. As much care as possible has been taken to see that the lists are complete and that any included dates are accurate. Apologies to all those helpers, assistants and part-timers who have not been acknowledged here.

Pastors (elders)
William E. Payne (Oct 72–June 97)
Carl Muller (Feb 98–April 21)
Josh Mills (Oct 21–present)

Associate pastors
Carl Muller (Oct 90–Feb 98)
Josh Mills (Sept 20–Oct 21)

Elders
At the founding of the church the following men were appointed as elders on January 5, 1973:

Hugh Clarke (73–77)   John Haughie (73)
Bob Wilkins (73–75)   Roy Schaub (73–75)

Since that time, the following men have served faithfully in this position of leadership:

Dr. Colin Wellum (73–09)   Bert Veldman (98–99)
Dr. Robert Duez (75 - 76)   Michael Haykin (98–07)
Don Wheaton (76–85)   Harry Droogendyk (00–04, 08–present)
Roy Thomson (76–88)   Steve Swallow (04–09)
George Fager (77–85)   Jonathan Wellum (05–present)
Geoff Oprel (86–87)   Gordon Vander Pol (09–13)
Mark Hudson (86–05, 06–20)   AJ Whitehead (10–21)
Wilf Ball (88–07)   Josh Mills (20–present)
Carl Muller (90–21)

Deacons
At the founding of the church the following men were appointed as deacons on January 5, 1973:

Jack Brouwers (73–75)   Dale Wilson (73–75)
Bob Clarke (73–75)

Since that time, the following men have served faithfully in this position of leadership:

Bruce Langford (74–76)   Joe Schofield (78–92, 99–21)
Fred Hambides (75–87, 93–97)   Bob Draper (78–80, 82–84)
Robert Laing (75–82, 86–93)   Mark Hudson (79–86)
John Skinner (76–79)   Roy Schaub (80–84)

Joe Vandenberg (82–93)
Geof Oprel (84–86)
Hank Veenvliet (87–96)
Jeroon Van de Merwe (92–96, 00–04)
Rick Thibault (93–99)
Roland Seiler (96–99)
Ian Richards (96–09)
Ron Walker (98–00)
Mark Payne (98–99)
Arjan Van de Merwe (99–01)
Matthew Richards (01–04)
Rick Egelton (01–04)
Gordon Vander Pol (02–06)
Nick Dunne (93–98, 04–05)
Dave Plante (05–17)
Fred Vlietstra (05–10, 12–16)
Darrin Brooker (06–10)
Joel Thibault (07–08)
Ding Macapagal (07–15)
Tim Brokking (08–12)
Henry Van Beek (08–12)
Scott Spencer (08–21)
John Van Leeuwen (09–12)
Frank Nickel (10–14)
Jeremy Schofield (10–21)
Adam Reynolds (12–16)
Justin Dokter (14–present)
Nathan Droogendyk (15–present)
Troy Regala (16–present)
Henry Heersink (17–21)
Jonathan Sommer (19–22)
Aric Verduyn (21–present)
Jesse van de Merwe (22–present)
Lewis Tuininga (22–present)

Administrative assistant
Matthew Richards (06–10)
Mark Hudson (11–20)

Church clerk (secretary)
Marjorie Pearce (72–73)
Jean Laing (73–18)
Mark Hudson (18–20)

Cradle roll
Joan Wellum (72–present!)

Envelope steward
Bob Clark (Feb 73–75)
Fred Hambides (75–78)
Bob Draper (78–91)
Roland Seiler (91–98)
Nick Dunne (98–05)
Darrin Brooker (05–10)
Ding Macapagal (10–15)
Nathan Droogendyk (15–present)

Fire marshall
Mark Hudson
Mark Payne
Gordon Vander Pol
Jeremy Schofield

Kids Club
Pastor & Hetty Payne
Wilf & Jackie Ball
Ruth Schofield
Mark & Carolyn Payne
Mark & Merry-Lynn Hudson
Aric Verduyn, Jessica Whitehead
Rick Thibault
Dave & Amy Plante
Nathan Droogendyk,
    Jeremy Schofield, Caitlin Muller
Nathan Droogendyk,
    Ira Regala, Johanna Wellum

Ladies Bible study
Michelle Veldman
Carolyn Egelton
Heather Muller
Karen Van Zanden, Heidi Wellum

Ladies fellowship
Hetty Payne
Merry-Lynn Hudson
Heather Muller, Heidi Wellum, Betty Vlietstra, Trudy Droogendyk

Librarians
Hugh Clarke
Linda Leggett
Rod Freeman
Alan Slaughter
John Kleingeld
Grace Thibault
Stephen Payne
Doug Van Zanden
Merry-Lynn Hudson
Sarah Van Hartingsveldt
Fernando Santana dos Santos

Maple Villa ministry
Carl Muller & family
Rachel Steenhof (Thibault), Janice Van Eck
Paul Goodfellow
AJ Whitehead & family, Scott Spencer

Missions secretary
Flo Walker
Catherine Van der Pol
Ruth Richards
Rick Thibault
Merry-Lynn Hudson
Roger Fellows
Heidi Wellum

Appendix 2: Key positions of service & leadership 187

Musicians
Lois Brouwers
Dorothy Wheaton
Eloise Meikle
Susan Meikle (Seiler)
Jan Draper (Oprel)
Merry-Lynn Hudson
Audrey Steenhof (Mead)
Rachel Steenhof (Thibault)
Jessica Whitehead
AJ Whitehead
Caitlin Muller
Harry Droogendyk
Sarah Van Hardingsveldt
Lyndsay Dokter
Eva Branda
Naomi Brokking
Emma Brokking
Kyla Mills

Sunday School superintendents
Bruce Langford (73–78)
Roy Thomson (78–82)
Kelvin Glass (82)
Joe Schofield (82–90)
Hank Veenvliet (90–96)
Gordon Vander Pol (96–09)
Tim Brokking (09–present)

Recording ministry
Rod Freeman
Jerry Wheaton
John Kleingeld
Alan Slaughter
Steve Payne
Bruce Walker
Paul Anderson
Jacob Kwakernaak
Bert Kooyman
Henry Heersink
Jonathan Sommer
David Wellum

Treasurers
Hugh Clarke (72–73)
Jack Brouwers (73–75)
Robert Laing (75–82, 86–93)
Robert Draper (82–84)
Geof Oprel (84–86)
Nick Dunne (93–98)
Ian Richards (98–08)
Scott Spencer (08–21)
Aric Verduyn (21–present)

Trustees
Fred Hambides
Roy Schaub
Roy Thomson
Dr. Colin Wellum
Nick Dunne
Gordon Vander Pol
Scott Spencer
David Plante
Justin Dokter

Young Adults / College & Careers

Carl & Heather Muller
Michael & Alison Haykin
Stephen & Karen Swallow

AJ & Jessica Whitehead
Harry & Trudy Droogendyk

Youth Group

Dale & Claudette Wilson, Bob & Jean Laing
Joe & Ruth Schofield
Mark & Merry-Lynn Hudson
Steven & Alison Payne, Rob & Kim Kilgour
Arjan & Betty VandeMerwe
Harry & Trudy Droogendyk
Daniel & Rachel Thibault
Derrick & Carolyn Lammers
Dave & Amy Plante
Jonathan & Heidi Wellum
Josh & Kyla Mills

Appendix 3

Missionary support

The year indicates when support started.

1973 Hugh and Jean Gordon (Pakistan)
1973 Peter and Chris Green (Philippines)
1975 Joan Brown (Ethiopia, through the Pioneer girls)
1975 Terry and Gail Tiessen (Philippines)
1978 David and Norma Surpless and family (Puerto Rico)
1982 Peter and Anna Pikkert (Middle East)
1984 Wilf and Jackie Ball (Zaire)
1987 Ed Wynne (Northern Ontario—Ojibway nation)
1987 Dr. Julie Stuffins (Pakistan)
1990 Michael and Maha Ghiz (Lebanon)
1991 Joost and Cheryl Pikkert (Indonesia)
1999 Roland and Susan Seiler (Mozambique then South Africa)

2005   Larry and Kathy Dunne (Ireland)
2006   Marco and Claudia Van de Merwe (Fazenda Immanuel, Brazil)
2009   Harry and Joy Bergen (Turkey)
2010   Haniel and Michelle Davy (Turkey)
2017   Matt and Ashley Klockenga, Ron and Jen Keres
        (Cat Lake, Northern Ontario)
2021   Nick and Courtney Platt (South-East Asia)

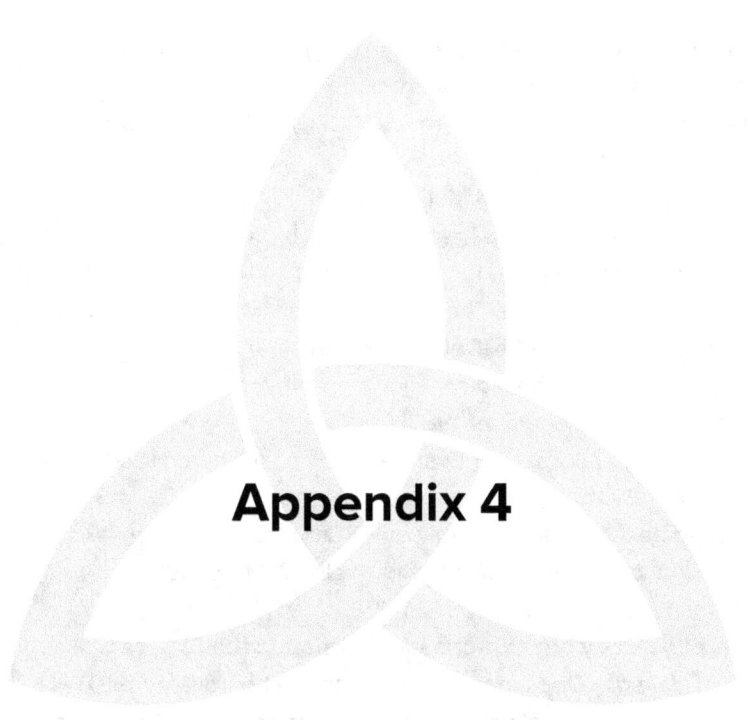

Appendix 4

Firsts, buildings & church support

◇◇◇◇◇◇◇◇

Some significant firsts at Trinity:

- official service (Sunday October 15, 1972)
- official offering (Sunday November 13, 1972)
- member to be married—Miss Marjorie Pearce to Mr. Lloyd Drury on Saturday, September 8, 1973. The service was performed by Pastor Payne at Stanley Avenue Baptist Church, Hamilton
- baptisms—Bob & Jean Laing (April 15, 1973)
- baby born—Cynthia Leigh Van Zanden (November 11, 1973)
- ministry reports presented at the Annual General Business Meeting (October 1975)
- service in the church building on Appleby Line (Sunday, February 28, 1976)
- wedding in the new building—Wilf & Jackie Ball (May 15, 1976)
- anniversary in the church building (fourth anniversary—October 17, 1976)

- ... College & Careers class (September 1977)
- ... watch night service (December 31, 1978)
- ... Canadian Carey Family Conference (CCFC) @ Camp Shalom with Walter Chantry (August 1979)
- ... message preached by Carl Muller (July 15, 1979)
- ... FRPS Pastor's Conference held at Westboro Baptist Church in Ottawa (Pastor Jim Clemens) with keynote speaker Dr. Al Martin (April 1980)
- ... regional prayer meetings—held in Burlington, Milton and Waterdown during the winter months (December 1981)
- ... evening meeting of the ladies fellowship (November 17, 1983)
- ... men's breakfast (December 1983)
- ... SGF picnic and rally at Blair Evangelical Baptist Church (Carl Muller) (September 22, 1984)
- ... church to be supported monthly by TBC ($500 per month)—Bright's Grove Community church near Sarnia (Kirk Wellum) (March 1985)
- ... Missions Weekend (March 23–24, 1985)
- ... ladies Bible study group proposed and started (1985)
- ... copy of *Ultimate Questions* presented to the board (May 1987)
- ... meeting to plan a local crisis pregnancy centre, chaired by Pastor Payne (September 1987)
- ... issue of *Trinity Times* (September 1990)
- ... assistant pastor—Carl Muller (October 1990)
- ... gift to support Carey Outreach Ministries—(Bob Penhearow) (November 1996)
- ... children's talk by Gord Vanderpol (January 12, 2003)
- ... service in the "new wing" (June 13, 2004)
- ... photo directory distributed (April 2007)
- ... Camp Courageous for kids (April 2009)
- ... weekly prayer item for the persecuted churches submitted for the bulletin by Sarah Pottruff (April 2011)
- ... major fire, forcing the church to relocate to alternate locations (August 2017)
- ... live video feed of service (October 2019)
- ... Covid-19 impacted service resulting in masks, hand-washing and social distancing (Spring 2020)
- ... official use of newly constructed original wing (February 2021)
- ... adoption of *Hymns of Grace* as the new church hymnal (June 2022)

Meeting locations and major church renovation/building:

- October 8 and 11, 1972, at 733 Ashley Ave., Burlington, Ont. (the home of John and Wilma Haughie)
- October 15, 1972–January 28, 1973, at Trefoil Lodge, Burlington
- February 4, 1973–December 2, 1973, at Central Public School, Brant St., Burlington
- September 12, 1973—Wednesday evenings at John A. Lockhart Public School for church activities
- December 9, 1973–February 21, 1976, at Trinity Christian School, Burlington
- February 28, 1976—the church building on Appleby Line for the first service
- February 22, 1987—dedication of the new addition of office, washrooms, nursery and prayer meeting room
- June 13, 2004—opening service in the new wing
- September 11, 2004—official dedication of the new wing
- August 2017–March 2018—meeting at Crossroads Centre, North Service Rd., Burlington, for Sunday services due to the fire
- August 2017–October 2019—meeting at St. George's Anglican, Palladium Way, Burlington, for prayer meetings, special meetings, ladies' Bible studies
- March 2018–October 2019—meeting at Ebenezer Canadian Reformed Church, Dynes Rd., Burlington, for Sunday services
- October 27, 2019—first service back in the partially restored church building
- February 2021—opening of the fellowship hall and classrooms of the rebuilt wing

Churches receiving regular financial support from Trinity for a defined period of time:

Blair Community Church (Cambridge; Carl Muller, Geof Oprel, Ron Matthews, David Robinson)
Grace Bible Church (Heritage College, Cambridge; David Robinson)
Sovereign Grace Community Church (Sarnia; Kirk Wellum)
Grace Baptist Church (Elmvale; Dale Nevelizer)
Beresford Baptist Church (Thunder Bay)
Église Evangélique Baptiste de Plessisville (Plessisville, Que.; Daniel Bernier)
Église Baptiste Évangélique des Laurentides (Laurentide, Que.; Raymond Perron)

Église Reformée de Charlesbourg
Trinity Baptist Church (Quispamsis, New Bruns.; Peter Dyck)
Westminster Baptist Chapel (London; Brian Robinson)
Grace Fellowship Church (Toronto; Paul Martin)
Faith Baptist Church (Scarborough; Brian Robinson)
Pilgrim Baptist Fellowship (Hamilton; Hagop Tchobanian)
Sovereign Grace Family Church (Belleville; Cliff Linnard)

Appendix 5

Motto texts

◇◇◇◇◇◇◇◇

Overall: "For I have not shunned to declare to you the whole counsel of God" (Acts 20:27).

2001	Matthew 19:26b	2012	Matthew 28:19b
2002	Mark 5:19	2013	John 20:21
2003	Colossians 4:2	2014	Matthew 6:33
2004	Matthew 6:9b	2015	Isaiah 55:11
2005	John 13:34	2016	2 Timothy 2:9b
2006	Matthew 5:14, 16	2017	2 Timothy 4:1–2
2007	2 Thessalonains 3:1	2018	Isaiah 46:10b
2008	2 Peter 3:18	2019	1 Samuel 12:24
2009	John 13:35	2020	John 2:17
2010	Philippians 1:21	2021	Matthew 6:10
2011	Ephesians 5:18	2022	Philippians 3:12–16

Appendix 6

Church anniversary speakers

◇◇◇◇◇◇◇◇

1973	William Payne	Trinity Baptist Church, Burlington, Ont.
1974	George Olley	Southgate Bible Truth Church, Ottawa, Ont.
1975	Robert Crooks	St. Andrews Presbyterian Church, Parry Sound, Ont.
1976	Eric Gurr	Jarvis Street Baptist Church, Toronto, Ont.
1977	Jim Clemens	Westboro Baptist Church, Ottawa, Ont.
1978	John Reisinger	Longbranch Baptist Church, Etobicoke, Ont.
1979	Liam Goligher	Hespler Baptist Church, Cambridge, Ont.
1980	Bob Wilkins	New Dundee Baptist Church, New Dundee, Ont.
1981	Roger Fellows	Bowmanville Baptist Church, Bowmanville, Ont.
1982	Al Martin	Trinity Baptist Church, Essex Falls, N.J., USA
1983	Norman Street	Jarvis Street Baptist Church, Toronto, Ont.
1984	Martin Holdt	Constantia Park Baptist Church, South Africa
1985	R.J. Reed	Toronto Baptist Seminary, Toronto, Ont.
1986	Stuart Olyott	France & Switzerland

Year	Speaker	Church/Institution
1987	Walter Chantry	Grace Baptist Church, Carlisle, Pa., USA
1988	Tom Nettles	Southern Baptist Theological Seminary, Louisville, Ky., USA
1989	Carl Muller	Trinity Baptist Church, Burlington, Ont.
1990	John Campbell	Albany Baptist Church, Brisbane, West Australia
1991	Kirk Wellum	Sovereign Grace Community Church, Sarnia, Ont.
1992	Earl Blackburn	Trinity Baptist Church, Los Angeles, Calif., USA
1993	William Payne	Trinity Baptist Church, Burlington, Ont.
1994	Martin Holdt	Constantia Park Baptist Church, South Africa
1995	Leigh Powell	Covenant Baptist Church, Toronto, Ont.
1996	John Campbell	Albany Baptist Church, Brisbane, West Australia
1997	Earl Blackburn	Trinity Baptist Church, Los Angeles, Calif., USA
1998	Roger Fellows	Leyton Drive Chapel, Bradford, UK
1999	Don Whitney	Midwestern Theological Seminary, Kansas City, Mo., USA
2000	Fred Zaspel	Word of Life Baptist Church, Pottsville, Pa., USA
2001	Kirk Wellum	Sovereign Grace Community Church, Sarnia, Ont.
2002	Martin Holdt	Constantia Park Baptist Church, South Africa
2003	Bob Penhearow	Grace Trinity Community Church, Guelph, Ont.
2004	Erroll Hulse	Leeds, UK; co-founder of African Pastors' Conferences, South Africa
2005	Jim Elliff	Christian Communicators Worldwide, Parkville, Mo., USA
2006	Kirk Wellum	Pilgrim Baptist Fellowship, Ancaster, Ont.
2007	Mark Webb	Grace Bible Church, Olive Branch, Miss., USA
2008	Richard Valade	Essex Baptist Church, Ont.
2009	Paul Martin	Grace Fellowship Church, Toronto, Ont.
2010	Bill Hughes	Emmanuel Baptist Church, Coconut Creek, Fla., USA
2011	Brian Robinson	Faith Baptist Church, Scarborough, Ont.
2012	Earl Blackburn	Heritage Baptist Church, Shreveport, La., USA
2013	Stephen Kring	Bethesda Baptist Church, Delhi, Ont.
2014	Don Theobald	Binbrook Baptist Church, Binbrook, Ont.
2015	Mark Webb	Grace Bible Church, Olive Branch, Miss., USA
2016	Steve West	Crestwicke Baptist Church, Guelph, Ont.
2017	Jeremy Walker	Maidenbower Baptist Church, Crawley, UK
2018	Bill Hughes	Christ Church, Deeside, Wales
2019	Joel Beeke	Heritage Reformed Congregation, Grand Rapids, Mich., USA

2020 Richard Valade   Essex, Ont.
2021 Alex Kloosterman Hill City Baptist Church, Peterborough, Ont.
2022 Stephen Wellum   Southern Baptist Theological Seminary,
                       Louisville, Ky., USA

Appendix 7

Cradle roll: Babies born at Trinity

◇◇◇◇◇◇◇◇

1. Cynthia Van Zanden (11.10.73)
2. Brenda Lively (16.03.74)
3. Sara Leggett (27.06.74)
4. Jonathan Langford (01.02.75)
5. Brian Van Zanden (09.02.75)
6. John Grant (23.10.75)
7. Stephen Laing (13.04.76)
8. Allan Wartlick (21.07.76)
9. Kathy Freeman (03.06.77)
10. Leslie Hudson (27.06.77)
11. Robert Freeman (19.08.78)
12. Laurie Hudson (29.06.79)
13. Colleen Ball (21.07.79)
14. Daniel Thibault (31.07.79)
15. Neil Davis (22.01.80)
16. Jonathan Laing (18.04.80)
17. Sarah Schofield (09.12.80)
18. Rebecca Wellum (13.05.81)
19. Joanne Ball (20.05.81)
20. Joel Thibault (26.08.81)
21. Jonathan Payne (14.09.82)
22. Jessica Ball (29.04.83)
23. David Thibault (27.05.84)
24. Brian Oprel (30.06.84)
25. Glenn Payne (13.11.84)
26. Blake Dendekker (16.06.85)
27. Alexandria Davis (24.06.85)
28. Jeremy Schofield (27.06.85)

29. Daniel Turner	(03.10.85)	67. Shane Van De Merwe	(20.03.95)
30. Matthew Payne	(10.11.86)	68. Amber Schenk	(18.09.95)
31. Benjamin Veenvliet	(15.11.86)	69. Gabriel Bylsma	(05.11.95)
32. Rebecca Nayler	(02.10.87)	70. Aemelia Mead	(06.12.95)
33. Andre Turner	(07.10.87)	71. Macayla Vander Pol	(06.04.96)
34. Jason Veenvliet	(23.05.88)	72. William Brand	(12.08.96)
35. Marissa Van de Merwe	(31.05.88)	73. Colin Dunne	(03.11.96)
36. Owen Pikkert	(31.07.88)	74. Janelle Van Leeuwen	(06.11.96)
37. Paul Sway	(03.10.88)	75. John Mark Veldman	(10.12.96)
38. Joel Van Beek	(15.01.89)	76. Curtis Plante	(24.01.97)
39. Caitlin Muller	(01.01.90)	77. McKenzie Haughie	(05.02.97)
40. Rita Pikkert	(01.06.90)	78. Taylor Schenk	(28.03.97)
41. Craig Van de Merwe	(08.07.90)	79. Jack Mead	(30.04.97)
42. Victor De Jong	(04.09.90)	80. Martin Goodfellow	(29.09.97)
43. Jeffrey Van Leeuwen	(18.10.90)	81. Victoria Brand	(19.11.97)
44. Amanda Van Beek	(03.11.90)	82. Ryk Vander Pol	(10.01.98)
45. Kyle Sway	(15.12.90)	83. Claire Van Zanden	(22.02.98)
46. Kevin Veenvliet	(13.05.91)	84. Emily Dunne	(19.08.98)
47. Deanna Harwood	(16.05.91)	85. Levi Schenk	(30.10.98)
48. Aaron Dendekker	(26.12.91)	86. Micah Van Beek	(09.01.99)
49. Julia Beerman	(25.07.92)	87. Michael Verduyn	(02.04.99)
50. Josh Van de Merwe	(26.09.92)	88. Samuel Goodfellow	(17.05.99)
51. Jenna Van Leeuwen	(14.05.93)	89. Samuel Berendse	(10.09.99)
52. Timothy Romyn	(17.05.93)	90. Ocean Powell	(13.09.99)
53. Luke Van Beek	(25.06.93)	91. Alexis Plante	(27.09.99)
54. Elsa Mead	(21.07.93)	92. Declan Haughie	(23.11.99)
55. Jesse Van de Merwe	(05.08.93)	93. Nadia Walker	(20.05.00)
56. Justin Steenhof	(02.09.93)	94. Jacob Crawford	(29.06.00)
57. David Muller	(07.12.93)	95. Wyatt Vander Pol	(19.07.00)
58. Rachel Beerman	(30.12.93)	96. Anthony Pascall	(11.08.00)
59. Alexander Bylsma	(31.01.94)	97. Katherine Erochko	(14.11.00)
60. Evan Dunne	(05.02.94)	98. North Powell	(27.12.00)
61. Meagan Payne	(03.05.94)	99. Xavier Thibault	(26.06.01)
62. Matthew Berendse	(13.06.94)	100. Caleb Vlietstra	(19.09.01)
63. Ellen Mead	(18.08.94)	101. Hannah Goodfellow	(13.02.02)
64. Bethany Payne	(17.10.94)	102. Reid Brooker	(12.10.02)
65. Varich De Jong	(11.11.94)	103. Caleb Walker	(18.09.03)
66. Connor Kilgour	(05.03.95)	104. Hudson Thibault	(20.10.03)

Cradle roll: Babies born at Trinity

105. Lauryn Vander Pol	(22.10.03)		143. Jovie Dokter	(18.08.12)
106. Bethany Cline	(13.02.04)		144. Calvin Reynolds	(26.09.12)
107. Zoe Thibault	(10.03.04)		145. Timothy Hojny	(17.10.12)
108. Dylan Crawford	(16.07.04)		146. Marshall Droogendyk	(03.12.12)
109. Carter Egelton	(27.02.05)		147. Ian Schofield	(17.01.13)
110. Ethan Thibault	(25.05.05)		148. Ryzen Guillet	(15.02.13)
111. Leah Brokking	(22.03.06)		149. Abigayle Pottruff	(12.03.13)
112. Jorja Thibault	(20.04.06)		150. Brooke Whitehead	(27.04.13)
113. Christina Wellum	(13.06.06)		151. Titus Li	(14.11.13)
114. Nolan Egelton	(28.07.06)		152. Elisabeth Zwart	(30.01.14)
115. Holly Wheeler	(10.09.06)		153. Michael Mindzak	(01.02.14)
116. Riley Thibault	(03.01.07)		154. Timothy Reynolds	(23.03.14)
117. Petranka McCall	(22.04.07)		155. Mikhaila Thommy	(26.03.14)
118. Sadie Thibault	(17.05.07)		156. Kate Reynolds	(25.06.14)
119. Gideon Plante	(13.08.07)		157. Jude Dokter	(07.10.14)
120. Judah Plante	(13.08.07)		158. Magdalena Tadros	(14.01.15)
121. Jakob VanHartingsveldt	(23.10.07)		159. Luke Schofield	(19.02.15)
122. Sofia Thibault	(02.06.08)		160. Sophia Van de Merwe	(10.04.15)
123. Liam Egelton	(25.08.08)		161. Cerys Whitehead	(18.05.15)
124. Owen Vander Munnik	(31.08.08)		162. Celina Reynolds	(11.08.15)
125. Yeats Thibault	(17.09.08)		163. Alex Droogendyk	(16.08.15)
126. Nathanael Aurich	(16.12.08)		164. Sarah Thommy	(10.11.15)
127. Jovie Grant	(06.01.09)		165. Jairo Guillet	(10.02.16)
128. Evangeline Beuth	(01.03.09)		166. Charis Tchobanian	(07.10.16)
129. Jotham Whitehead	(23.09.09)		167. Zipporha dos Santos	(24.11.16)
130. Aiden VanHartinsgveldt	(27.11.09)		168. Emma Mindzak	(16.01.17)
131. Ethan Pottruff	(12.01.10)		169. William Van de Merwe	(06.04.17)
132. Liam Crawford	(17.03.10)		170. Ellen Schofield	(01.04.18)
133. Avalyn Vander Munnik	(28.07.10)		171. Abram Dokter	(17.06.20)
134. Hitomi Verhoeckx	(23.09.10)		172. Aceyn Vlietstra	(13.02.21)
135. Robert Richards	(06.10.10)		173. Krew Sommer	(15.02.21)
136. Elijah Reynolds	(29.10.10)		174. James Day	(25.02.21)
137. Georgia Reynolds	(04.02.11)		175. Andie Sommer	(25.09.21)
138. Levi Whitehead	(12.05.11)		176. Kal Tuininga	(03.10.21)
139. Jake Zwart	(24.01.12)		177. Ezra Hutton	(30.12.21)
140. Susanna Reynolds	(08.05.12)		178. Isaac Mills	(16.04.22)
141. Asher VanHartingsveldt	(17.06.12)			
142. Hannah Verhoeckx	(05.08.12)			

Appendix 8

What in the world happened in the...

◇◇◇◇◇◇◇◇

Perhaps a small sampling of significant events and creations that shaped the wider world would be helpful in establishing a broader context in which to observe the development of Trinity Baptist Church over the decades. As several chapters are delineated by decade, here is an overview of key events within those timeframes.

What in the world happened in the...

1970s
Watergate, Skylab is launched, *Roe v. Wade*, the murders at the 1972 Summer Olympics in Munich, end of the Vietnam war, the Apple computer, Three Mile Island, disco, *Star Wars* hits the big screen, test tube baby, Jonestown, launch of *Voyager* 1 and 2, China's one-child policy, world population reaches 4 billion.

1980s
Eruption of Mt. St. Helen's, the work of Lech Walesa in Poland, first orbital flight of the space shuttle, Prince Charles and Lady Diana Spencer marry, AIDS epidemic begins and HIV recognized as the cause, first CD player sold by Sony, DNA fingerprinting first used, *Challenger* and Chernobyl disasters, stock market crash, fall of the Berlin wall, Tiananmen Square massacre in China, world population reaches 5 billion.

1990s
The arrival of the World Wide Web, the launch of the Hubble space telescope, German reunification and the dissolution of the Soviet Union, the creation of the European Union, end of apartheid in South Africa, the opening of the channel tunnel, "Dolly" the sheep is cloned, OJ Simpson trial, Hong Kong now under Chinese rule, *Harry Potter*, Google, Columbine High School massacre, world population reaches 6 billion.

2000s
Y2K, 9/11 terrorist attacks, Indonesian tsunami, Hurricane Katrina, Virginia Tech massacre, SARS, space shuttle *Columbia*, Saddam Hussein, Iraq and Afghanistan wars, Al-Qaeda, H1N1, Mars Rover, GPS, USB flash drive, New Atheism, climate change, Avatar, *Lord of the Rings*, Xbox and PS2, Facebook, world population reaches 6.84 billion.

2010s
Arab Spring, LBGT rights increase, economic and military growth of China, trade wars, Osama bin Laden killed, rise of ISIS, annexation of Crimea by Russia, smartphones, cloud computing, 5G, WikiLeaks, #MeToo movement, global warming, Blackhawks win 3 Stanley Cups, Haiti earthquake, Sulawesi earthquake and tsunami, Hurricane Sandy, *Avengers: Endgame* at $2.7B, online streaming, Minecraft, SpaceX, self-driving cars, Higgs boson, Brexit, world population reaches 7.7 billion.

2020–2022
Covid-19, March meltdown in stocks, modified and mostly spectatorless pro sports (NBA bubble), lengthy lockdowns, USA and China on Mars at the same time, another Liberal minority govenment, Democrat Joe Biden is president of the USA, launch of WEBB telescope, Winter Olympics in Beijing, trucker convoy in Ottawa, Russia invades Ukraine, Canadian men to World Cup soccer.

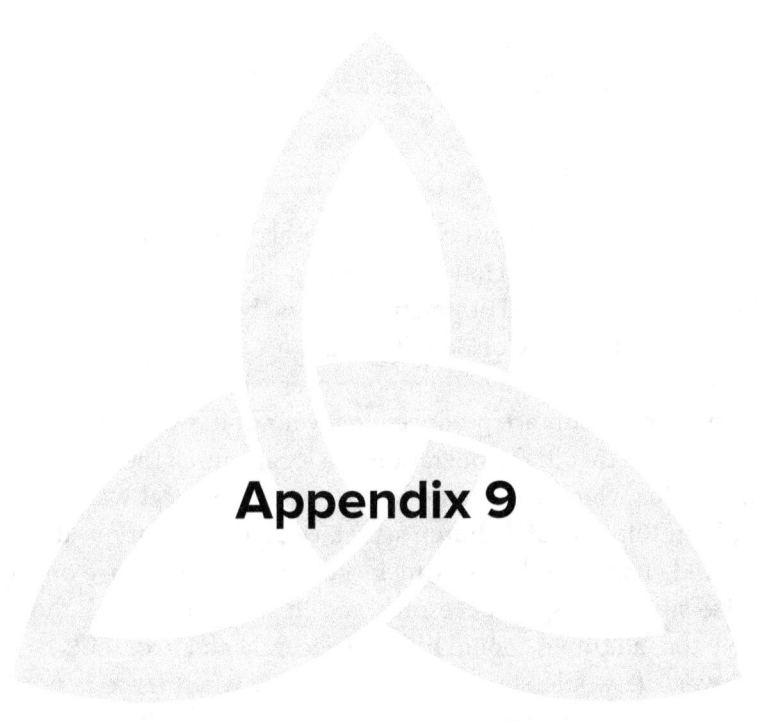

Appendix 9

What is a Reformed Baptist church?

◇◇◇◇◇◇◇◇

This is the essence of one of the first sermons preached by Pastor Bill Payne on the founding of Trinity Baptist Church. Its intent was to clarify the church's position on a number of critical issues.

What kind of a church are we building? What is a Reformed Baptist church?

If I were to be asked, "What kind of a church are you?" I would not hesitate to reply, "We are a Baptist church!" We hold to those truths which have sometimes been referred to as *Baptist distinctives*.

I would also reply, "We are a Reformed church," inasmuch as we hold to the great doctrines of the Reformation in the areas concerning the salvation of men. In this sense, I am not at all averse to our church being referred to as a *Reformed Baptist church*, and I want to speak on the subject, "What is a Reformed Baptist church?"

1. The Scriptures

First of all, a Reformed Baptist church is a local church which acknowledges the supreme authority of Holy Scripture. In all matters of faith, that is in the things we believe, and of practice, that is the things which we do, our sole authority is the Word of God. If something, whether of faith or of practice, is contrary to the Bible, then no matter who pleads for it, no matter what clever arguments are produced in favour of it, we cannot endorse it.

We recognize that in the operation of a local church there may be items introduced for which there may be no specific biblical warrant. For instance, I am thinking of a church secretary as an illustration. It would be hard to find chapter and verse which states we ought to have one, but we recognize such things are necessary, and in accordance with the biblical principle that all things should be done decently and in order.[1]

However, we would state emphatically that when there is no express biblical warrant for something, we are not going to look upon it as *sacred* and *binding*. When the Word of God does not warrant something, we are not going to be brought under bondage to it; but where the Scriptures clearly call for something, no consideration ought to make us do without it. We desire to have our conscience bound to the Word of God, for there we believe is true freedom. It is my opinion that a number of items in present day Baptist churches have no true biblical warrant. They are a part of the church because they were introduced some years ago and are now "Baptist tradition." Perhaps many people take it for granted that they are scriptural, but if they were challenged to produce scriptural evidence for these practices, they would be hard pressed to find any.

In other areas, there are things the Scriptures clearly call for and which have dropped out of most modern Baptist churches, and we ought to call for them to be brought back. The *eldership* would be an example of this point. Baptist churches used to have an eldership years ago; in most Baptist churches today you cannot find it. But we believe if we are going to be truly patterned on the New Testament churches, we need to return to the concept of eldership. The Scriptures present it; we ought to have it!

---

[1] 1 Corinthians 14:40.

So Reformed Baptists are not governed by tradition, not by the opinion of man, not by sentiment, nor by pragmatism, but by the Word of God alone. We believe in the authority of Scripture, and we desire in our church life to be patterned after and conformed to the Word of God. We should always be seeking for God to deepen our understanding of His Word, and we should always be ready to reform any of our practices if it becomes apparent we are out of line with the Scriptures. The attitude which says, "It doesn't matter what the Bible says, this is the way we have always done it," is to us frightening; indeed sinful. It must be "to the law and to the testimony"[2] or "what saith the Scriptures?"[3]

2. Preaching

Secondly, Reformed Baptists believe in the pre-eminence of the preaching of the Word of God. We believe the preaching of the Bible must have the central place in our services. We believe nothing can or should take the place of the preaching of the Word!

Our conviction is the church of Christ has suffered because she has downgraded the preaching of the Word. We believe seminaries and Bible colleges ought to be pre-eminently places where preachers are produced and encouraged. We believe God's people everywhere ought to be encouraged to pray that God would endow men with gifts of preaching, and He would give to His churches preachers, great preachers, many preachers. We believe there is a need in the churches of Christ for a fresh realization of the importance of the preaching of the Word of God, and that young men ought to be encouraged to study theology, church history and the sermons of great preachers of the past; they ought to work hard to become good preachers of the Bible.

In these days of increasing usage of films in services, and of increasing emphasis on musical programs, we desire to stress the pre-eminence of the preaching of the Word of God. We do not suggest these other things have no place in the churches, but we do insist they be clearly subservient to the preaching of the Scriptures.

---

[2] Isaiah 8:20.
[3] Romans 4:3.

3. The doctrines of grace

Thirdly, Reformed Baptists unashamedly declare their belief in those doctrines which are sometimes called the *doctrines of grace*. By this expression we mean in particular the doctrines of total depravity, unconditional election, definite atonement, effectual calling and the perseverance of the saints. We rejoice in those glorious truths which uphold the sovereignty of God in the salvation of men, and which so gloriously affirm the great central reality that salvation is all of grace, and salvation is of the Lord!

We rejoice that the doctrines of grace are clearly set forth in the *Second London Confession of Faith of 1689*, and in many other historic Baptist creeds. We note that in 1861, when Charles Spurgeon opened the great Metropolitan Tabernacle in London, England, he celebrated the occasion by having sermons preached by esteemed guests on each of those distinctive doctrines. And yet it is not because Spurgeon, or any other Baptist, preached these doctrines that we believe them. It is not just because these doctrines are found in the historic Baptist creeds, though we rejoice that is the case, but it is because the doctrines are so clearly presented in the Holy Scriptures that we believe them.

We recognize we live in an age when these great fundamental truths are ignored, and even blatantly denied by many professing the name *evangelical* and the name *Baptist*. We know they are unpopular truths, but truth they are, and we receive them and rejoice in them.

We would like to emphasize also that we not only believe them, but we further believe they ought to be clearly preached and taught from the pulpit! We have a tragic situation today when men in pulpits say they believe the doctrines of grace, but they refuse to preach and teach them to their people.

The result is churches are full of people uninstructed in the great truths of the Scriptures (and of the historic Baptist faith), and these people then imbibe the very opposite doctrines—which they easily receive over the radio and via religious periodicals. Often, when a man comes into such a congregation and preaches the truths of grace, uproar and opposition ensue. This is tragic, but common. We believe our day needs the doctrines of grace, and our people need to be instructed in them.

4. Evangelism

In the next place, we would like to affirm Reformed Baptists believe in the necessity and responsibility of evangelism. We have no more liking for Hyper-Calvinism than we have for Arminianism.

We do not believe there is an inconsistency between God's sovereignty in the salvation of His chosen people and His command to us to preach the gospel to every creature. If there seems to be a difficulty in our minds reconciling any of the truths of His Word, we see it as the result of the darkness of our own understanding, and we believe our duty is to obey the Word, whether we understand it all or not. We believe in evangelism!

Now it is true we do not believe in much that goes under the name of evangelism in this twentieth century. We believe much that is called evangelism today is little more than psychology and salesmanship; we are appalled by the superficial work which goes under the name of evangelism; we are appalled by the pressures, gimmicks and schemes, all calculated to produce "decisions" and impressive statistics, but which work such havoc in the souls of men. No!

Because we believe in evangelism, it does not mean we are going to cooperate with every scheme which bears that name. We believe that in evangelism, as in everything else, as we said earlier, we must be governed by the Word of God. The message of evangelism must be according to the Scriptures, and the method of evangelism must be governed by the Word of God! Nevertheless, we repeat, we *do* believe in evangelism, and our prayer is God would ever keep us mindful of the need to evangelize. May God ever give us a burden to evangelize, knowing it is for His glory and for the salvation of men.

We believe it is our responsibility to make known the gospel, first in our own community, and in Canada at large, and indeed in all the world. We believe in missions, home and foreign, and we believe we ought to seek the souls of men in every way that is consistent with the Word of God.

5. Worship

Finally, let me say a Reformed Baptist church is a local church with a serious approach to worship.

The God we worship is a God of majesty, glory and holiness. And the God of the Bible is One before whom the angels of heaven constantly cry,

"Holy, Holy, Holy" as they worship Him day and night[4]; "He is great and greatly to be praised."[5] We believe that when we come together to worship this great and glorious God of the Bible, we ought to do so with reverence and with godly fear. We believe there ought to be a sense of *awe* in our hearts when we gather to worship this God!

You say, "But surely there must be joy as well." Yes indeed, we agree, but equally surely it must be a joy which is *in God*; not a joy arising from some natural "good feeling," but a joy arising out of the knowledge of the Lord, and a joy tempered and controlled by reverence.

We believe there is a world of difference between a "dead" service and a serious, spiritual service. The first is not desired; the second is. Now because of this desire for serious worship, we believe anything which would detract from that ought not to be allowed among us. Frivolity and childishness seem to us to be out of place and incongruous with the worship of God.

We also believe music in the church ought to be governed by the great central fact of the One whom we worship. So much of the music invading the churches today seems little more than carnal imitation of the world. There is very little difference between what is presented on the church platform and what is presented on the television or the worldly floor show—except, of course, that "religious" words are uttered rather than "secular" ones. But this spirit is of the world; the appeal is to the flesh. This we abhor and reject as having no place in the worship of God. That which is sacred ought not to be prostituted and used as entertainment. If men want to be entertained, let them be honest enough to go to some secular hall of amusement and be entertained; let them not pretend to be worshipping or in a service when entertainment is the order of the day. No! When we gather to worship, we want to keep the world out; we want to appeal not to the flesh, but to the Spirit; we want not the sophistication of the world, but the simplicity of Christ. Oh, that when we worship we might feel the awe of the God in our souls! Oh, that we might see something of the glory seen by Isaiah[6] and by the servants of God of old!

This, then is the kind of church we are seeking to build. Other things could be said, but we have sought to touch on some of the basic points.

---

[4] See Revelation 4:8.
[5] Psalm 96:4.
[6] See Isaiah 6.

May God raise up many such churches all over the land and all over the world, which desire the same things and strive toward them. May God be pleased to visit His people again with showers of blessing[7] that God might be glorified in and through His church!

W.E. Payne

---

[7] See Ezekiel 34:26.

Deo Optimo et Maximo Gloria
To God, best and greatest, be glory

hesedandemet.com

www.ingramcontent.com/pod-product-compliance
Lightning Source LLC
Chambersburg PA
CBHW072049110526
44590CB00018B/3104